P9-DID-766

MAPS

Plotting Places on the Globe

These and other books are included in the Encyclopedia of Discovery and Invention series:

Airplanes	Microscopes
Anesthetics	Movies
Animation	Phonograph
Atoms	Photography
Automobiles	Plastics
Clocks	Plate Tectonics
Computers	Printing Press
Dinosaurs	Radar
Explosives	Radios
Genetics	Railroads
Germs	Ships
Gravity	Submarines
Guns	Telephones
Human Origins	Telescopes
Lasers	Television
Maps	Vaccines

Maps
Plotting Places on the Globe

by PAULA BRYANT PRATT

The ENCYCLOPEDIA of
D·I·S·C·O·V·E·R·Y
and INVENTION

P.O. Box 289011, SAN DIEGO, CA 92198-9011

Library of Congress Cataloging-in-Publication Data

Pratt, Paula, 1959-
  Maps: plotting places on the globe / by Paula Bryant Pratt.

    p. cm.—(The encyclopedia of discovery and invention)
  Includes bibliographical references and index.
  ISBN 1-56006-255-X
  1. Cartography—Juvenile literature.   [1. Cartography.
  2. Maps.]   I. Title.   II. Series.
  GA105.6.P72 1995
  912—dc20   94-18018
                                                     CIP
                                                     AC

Contents

■■

Foreword

The belief in progress has been one of the dominant forces in Western Civilization from the Scientific Revolution of the seventeenth century to the present. Embodied in the idea of progress is the conviction that each generation will be better off than the one that preceded it. Eventually, all peoples will benefit from and share in this better world. R.R. Palmer, in his *History of the Modern World*, calls this belief in progress "a kind of nonreligious faith that the conditions of human life" will continually improve as time goes on.

For over a thousand years prior to the seventeenth century, science had progressed little. Inquiry was largely discouraged, and experimentation, almost nonexistent. As a result, science became regressive and discovery was ignored. Benjamin Farrington, a historian of science, characterized it this way: "Science had failed to become a real force in the life of society. Instead there had arisen a conception of science as a cycle of liberal studies for a privileged minority. Science ceased to be a means of transforming the conditions of life." In short, had this intellectual climate continued, humanity's future would have been little more than a clone of its past.

Fortunately, these circumstances were not destined to last. By the seventeenth and eighteenth centuries, Western society was undergoing radical and favorable changes. And the changes that occurred gave rise to the notion that progress was a real force urging civilization forward. Surpluses of consumer goods were replacing substandard living conditions in most of Western Europe. Rigid class systems were giving way to social mobility. In nations like France and the United States, the lofty principles of democracy and popular sovereignty were being painted in broad, gilded strokes over the fading canvasses of monarchy and despotism.

But more significant than these social, economic, and political changes, the new age witnessed a rebirth of science. Centuries of scientific stagnation began crumbling before a spirit of scientific inquiry that spawned undreamed of technological advances. And it was the discoveries and inventions of scores of men and women that fueled these new technologies, dramatically increasing the ability of humankind to control nature—and, many believed, eventually to guide it.

It is a truism of science and technology that the results derived from observation and experimentation are not finalities. They are part of a process. Each discovery is but one piece in a continuum bridging past and present and heralding an extraordinary future. The heroic age of the Scientific Revolution was simply a start. It laid a foundation upon which succeeding generations of imaginative thinkers could build. It kindled the belief that progress is possible as long as there were gifted men and women who would respond to society's needs. When Antonie van Leeuwenhoek observed *Animalcules* (little animals) through his high-powered microscope in 1683, the discovery did not end there. Others followed who would call these "little animals" bacteria and, in time, recognize their role in the process of health and disease. Robert Koch, a German bacteriologist and winner of the Nobel Prize in Physiology and Medicine, was one of these men. Koch firmly established that bacteria are responsible for causing infectious diseases. He identified, among others, the causative organisms of anthrax and tuberculosis. Alexander Fleming, another Nobel Laureate, progressed still further in the quest to understand and control bacteria. In 1928, Fleming discovered penicillin, the antibiotic wonder drug. Penicillin, and the generations of antibiotics that succeeded it, have done more to

prevent premature death than any other discovery in the history of humankind. And as civilization hastens toward the twenty-first century, most agree that the conquest of van Leeuwenhoek's "little animals" will continue.

The *Encyclopedia of Discovery and Invention* examines those discoveries and inventions that have had a sweeping impact on life and thought in the modern world. Each book explores the ideas that led to the invention or discovery, and, more importantly, how the world changed and continues to change because of it. The series also highlights the people behind the achievements—the unique men and women whose singular genius and rich imagination have altered the lives of everyone. Enhanced by photographs and clearly explained technical drawings, these books are comprehensive examinations of the building blocks of human progress.

MAPS

Plotting Places on the Globe

MAPS

Introduction

Maps are a kind of coded language, a way of showing people where they are. People have communicated using maps for thousands of years, probably since humans first became aware of the world.

Maps have come a long way since early cave dwellers traced lines in the dirt with sticks. Gradually, societies learned that they were not in the center of the universe. They began to explore their world. Maps helped guide them. Returning adventurers shared their discoveries graphically, in map form, and others were inspired to venture into the unknown lands surrounding them.

During the Renaissance, the idea of maps as scientific tools became widespread. Cartographers and surveyors worked together to discover the shape of the world in relation to its position in the universe. The first maps based on precise astronomical calculations were published during this time.

Scientific measurements continued to improve the accuracy of maps during the eighteenth and nineteenth centuries. Nations began to work together to plot detailed maps of their own coastlines and interiors. Maps thus became a way of defining shared cultures.

Now, fleets of satellites hover above

... TIMELINE: MAPS

1 > 2 > 3 > 4 > 5 > 6 > 7 >

1 ■ 6th Century
Babylonian world map drawn on clay tablet.

2 ■ ca. 200 B.C.
Eratosthenes calculates circumference of earth.

3 ■ ca. 150 B.C.
Hipparchus first uses longitude and latitude.

4 ■ A.D. 127- ca. 145
Claudius Ptolemy, mathematician, astronomer, and cartographer, publishes his major works in Alexandria.

5 ■ 15th Century
Ptolemy's *Geography* revived in Europe.

6 ■ 1492
Columbus reaches the New World.

7 ■ 1569
Mercator publishes new map projection.

8 ■ 1696
Completion of the scientifically compiled world map, the *planisphére terrestre*, at the Paris Observatory.

9 ■ 1700
Jean-Dominique Cassini begins national survey of France.

10 ■ 1735-1744
French expeditions to Lapland and Peru prove that the earth is flattened at the poles.

11 ■ 1762
John Harrison's Number 4 chronometer determines accurate longitude.

12 ■ 1787
Triangulation across the English Channel links British and French national surveys.

the planet, quietly collecting data that they beam down to huge computer systems on earth. Maps compiled from this information are far more specialized and precise than ever before. Mapping has become one of the first truly global efforts.

The high-technology maps of today hold implications for the future. Seismologists can use computerized maps to help predict earthquakes. Military and commercial airplanes can fly more safely and efficiently thanks to precise flight patterns derived from computers and orbiting satellites. Computerized data bases allow anyone to access maps tailored to specific needs, such as determining the environmental impact of a proposed construction project.

No map is a complete picture. Each map shows just a part of the puzzle of life on earth, drawn according to the mapmaker's own ideas. Maps are powerful tools: they can guide ships and jumbo jets, locate soldiers in vast deserts, warn researchers about the location of possible earthquakes, show scientists the planet's changing face from the sky. They can convey more facts at a glance than any written document. If people are educated about what maps can and cannot do, then humanity is on the way to employing them as exciting tools to steer the world into the future.

13 ■ 1791
Beginning of British Ordnance Survey.

14 ■ 1793
Completion of France's Carte de Cassini, the first scientifically conducted national survey.

15 ■ 1804-1806
Lewis and Clark survey the American West by land.

16 ■ 1879
U.S. Geological Survey founded.

17 ■ 1884
Greenwich meridian named the prime meridian at international conference.

18 ■ 1972
Landsat 1 launched by United States.

19 ■ 1980
USGS completes survey.

20 ■ 1986
First SPOT satellite launched by France.

21 ■ 1990s
Global Positioning System becomes operational.

Mapping Earth's Place in the Universe

People have always wanted to know where they stand in relation to the world around them. Humans have an inborn sense of space, instinctively grasping the concepts of distance and direction. The mapping instinct, the urge to record one's place in the world, is primal. Even prehistoric people are thought to have turned the acute awareness of their surroundings into map form, outlining their impressions onto stone or animal skin. These prehistoric maps must have looked very different from the maps used today. But all maps have one thing in common: Maps turn physical space into a kind of abstract code. Like words, all the symbols that make up a map stand for objects or ideas. In many societies, people drew maps before they invented mathematics or written language. Like language, mapping is a kind of communication. Maps tell how people see their world.

The Omphalos Syndrome

Most early civilizations were sure that everything revolved around themselves. Societies that believe they are at the

This ancient Mesopotamian map shows Babylon at the center of the world. Throughout the centuries, people have used maps to illustrate their myths and legends instead of conveying detailed factual information.

Although prehistoric peoples did not record their histories, it is likely that they used crude maps to tell each other of favorite hunting spots.

world's center are said to have the omphalos syndrome. ("Omphalos" is from the Greek word for navel.) This worldview may seem self-important. But it is also a natural outlook, stemming from "a basic human response: Here I am, and I stand at the heart of all that is around me," as writers Simon Berthon and Andrew Robinson put it. Cartographers, or mapmakers, have struggled against the attraction of the omphalos syndrome for many centuries. They try to design maps that represent the world as it is, not just as people would like it to be.

An Expanding Worldview

Primitive humans comfortably assigned themselves a secure place on earth.

Then they began to test its boundaries. Prehistoric tribe members needed to venture away from home to gather food or to hunt. Periodically, they discovered new places to find water, salt, or game. If they wanted to remember how to get there again, or if they wanted to direct other tribe members there, they might have drawn maps of the path on the skin of an animal or on a cave wall. If they needed to visit a neighboring tribe, or to avoid the camps of enemy tribes they might have traced maps in the dirt that showed others around the campfire the enemy's direction and distance from their own tribe's camp. Mapping meant sharing facts with fellow tribespeople about things like food and shelter that were basic to everyone's survival.

Gradually, primitive peoples became nomadic, wandering from place to place. Their mobility expanded the horizons of their worldview. Once-familiar surroundings became new and different. The farther they ventured, the more important maps became. Detailed maps could help them keep track of where they fit in a changing landscape. Writer Lloyd A. Brown speculates that

> wandering tribes needed to know how to cross the desert without dying of thirst and how to get home after grazing their flocks for many miles during the summer season. Making war, an ancient method of acquiring land, meant knowing your neighbor's territory and not forgetting it.

Early Traders and Maps

Maps became especially desirable as nomadic peoples began to trade with one another, exchanging valuables like spices, tin, and amber. From around 1100 to 700 B.C., the Phoenicians were famous traders. They alone were bold enough to leave their homeland (in the western portion of what is currently Lebanon) and sail their oared vessels across the Mediterranean and into the Atlantic Ocean, much farther than the Greeks, Egyptians, or Persians dared to sail. These ancient navigators are fabled to have sailed completely around the coast of Africa approximately two thousand years before the Portuguese achieved the same feat. The Phoenicians, known as "red men" because their skins were weather-beaten from exposure to sun and wind while at sea, kept the records of their trade routes secret because they wanted to block competition for their Northern Euro-

Sturdy ships like this vessel dating from the seventh century B.C. allowed the Phoenicians to sail farther and over longer periods of time than did other early peoples. Although their records no longer exist, it seems likely that they would have drawn maps to guide their journeys.

Phoenician traders were the most adventurous of their neighbors and were very secretive about their valuable trade routes.

pean tin trading. Although the Phoenicians' records are lost to us, it is unlikely that they accomplished such lengthy journeys well beyond sight of shore without the aid of maps to guide them. Ancient Greek mapmakers, eager for knowledge only an explorer could experience firsthand, would later try to reconstruct this seafaring people's bold journeys to help them fit together the puzzle of what lay on the earth's face beyond familiar shores.

Thus trading became an important way to learn about the world, and early navigators cooperated, at least with each other, to create increasingly accurate maps of their routes. Brown comments on the role of early trade in the progress of mapmaking:

> Commerce with other tribes and nations meant knowing still more about distance and direction; the farther away the markets the more accurate the routes to and from them had to be. Dis-

tance and direction became increasingly important as civilization expanded, and . . . geographical accounts and pictures, the way to get from place to place, were set down—after a fashion—on stone, papyrus and parchment. Few of them survived.

The Scarcity of Early Maps

Many ancient maps lasted well into the pre-Christian era, but few of these exist today. This makes the history of cartography difficult for researchers to study. Why didn't early maps survive? According to Brown, "The very material used in the making of maps, charts and globes contributed to their destruction." Researchers have learned from historical accounts that maps were sometimes carved on silver, copper, or brass plates. In times of war, these could have fallen prey to looters and been melted down for the value of the metal.

Maps drawn on parchment could easily be scraped off so the parchment could be reused. Maps cut in stone could later end up as building material. In addition, maps often met with the same dire fates as the travelers who carried them. According to Brown:

> Ancient maps were designed primarily for travelers, soldiers and mariners. Traveling in ancient times was a hazardous business. . . . Highwaymen were as common as hostels were rare; consequently many "traveler's pictures," road maps and itineraries rotted by the wayside with their owners' bodies. Fire, flood and shipwreck accounted for many more.

Another reason that few early maps survive is that many empires regarded maps as secret messages that could reveal dangerous information if they fell into the wrong hands. As Brown points out:

> Maps and charts have always been surrounded by an aura of mystery and secrecy which has had much to do with their destruction, and retarded at the same time the dissemination of geographic knowledge. They were dangerous things to have around. . . . Because they were potential sources of information to the enemy, maps of an empire or even a city were closely guarded.

Among the military secrets that maps could reveal were the locations of roads and navigable streams that could provide invaders entrance into a city. Once inside the city walls, a stolen map could easily help enemy troops find and occupy a city's arsenals, barracks, docks, and public buildings.

A final reason that ancient maps are hard to find is that, as new societies replaced old ones, old maps were discarded and new ones made. Successive civilizations exchanged old worldviews for new ones, and each society saw their own vision as the true one. In this process, knowledge acquired by one culture might be erased by the next society to dominate if the earlier culture's information conflicted with the new culture's idea of how the world should look.

World Maps and Worldviews

Despite the lack of ancient maps to examine, historical records give us a good idea of the way ancient civilizations saw the earth. Like prehistoric tribes, each civilization placed itself centrally. In addition, the ancient Egyptians, Babylonians, and even the early Greeks all saw the earth as flat. Their idea of a disklike

This clay tablet, measuring the size of a hand, is the oldest surviving map. Dating from the sixth century B.C., it depicts Babylon at the center of a flat, disklike world.

world surrounded by water echoes the primitive worldview of the earth as a circle extending only to the horizon line.

The oldest surviving world map was inscribed on a clay tablet in sixth-century B.C. Mesopotamia, a region of southwest Asia and home of one of the earliest civilizations on earth. The tablet measures only five by three inches, about the size of a hand. Pictured on it are two lines running across the center of a round, flat earth. These lines represent the Tigris and Euphrates Rivers of the Mesopotamian valley. In the middle of the circle is the walled city of Babylon. Encompassing everything is the Bitter River, filled with imaginary beasts. (The Babylonians believed that the world emerged from the body of Tiamat, the saltwater goddess, represented by the circular river on the map.)

As Simon Berthon and Andre Robinson point out, the ancient Babylonians could boast of a sophisticated knowledge of astronomy. And yet, when they pictured their world, they drew from their myths, not from their knowledge of science. Doing so "provided reassurance and comfort, whereas the uncertainties of science could have led to anxiety and disorientation. . . . It was to be the Greeks who first grappled with the reality of the cosmos."

The Early Greek and Chinese Worldviews

Eventually, the Greeks connected what they had learned about the stars with what they knew of the earth to make great strides toward the creation of an accurate world map. In the sixth century B.C., however, the Greek and Babylonian worldviews were remarkably similar.

In that century, Anaximander of Miletus is said to have been the first Greek to draw a world map. All copies of Anaximander's map have disappeared, but the way it looked has been reconstructed from later descriptions. Like the Babylonian world map, Anaximander's earth is a disk. Naturally, however, Greece rather than Babylon takes center stage. The river Okeanos flows around the earth's rim.

The ancient Chinese were just as eager as the Babylonians and the early Greeks to place their civilization at the universe's hub. China's name means "middle kingdom." Its early world maps reflected this view. According to writer Samuel Y. Edgerton Jr., the Chinese of the fifth century B.C. diagrammed their universe as a network of rectangles nested one within the other.

> The center of this "map" represents the imperial palace. Reading outward, the next rectangle represents the imperial domains; then the lands of the tributary nobles; then the zone of pacification where border peoples are adjusting to Chinese customs; then the land of friendly barbarians; and finally,

A re-creation of Anaximander's map of the world. Dating from the sixth century B.C. and depicting the earth as a disk, Anaximander's map places Greece at the disk's center, reflecting its creator's prejudices.

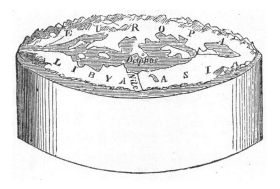

This remnant of a Greek omphalos once marked the center of the ancient city of Delphi.

the outermost rectangle separates Chinese civilization from the lands of savages who have no culture at all.

Edgerton explains that this orderly nest of boxes with its palace safely in the center must have made ancient Chinese map viewers feel sure that their ruler was safely protected.

City Plans and Worldviews

Early world maps were obviously not realistic replicas of the earth, but rather symbolic pictures of a society's views about itself. Basically, early peoples wanted to show their close relationship with heaven. As Edgerton points out, most civilizations built their cities to match their worldview. A favorite sym-

bol of ancient city planners was a raised monument, such as a tower, erected at a central crossroads. The monument's purpose was to link the community to heaven. The omphalos in the Greek city of Delphi was a sacred conical stone that marked the center of the Greek world. But Delphi's was not the only omphalos. Hundreds of other cities in Egypt, Mesopotamia, India, China, Africa, Europe, and the Americas displayed their own centrally placed monuments, showing that they too wanted to stress their cosmic significance when they built their cities.

This type of ordered city planning marked the transition from isolated tribe to conquering civilization.

According to Edgerton, the phenomenon of planning cities to suit the cosmos "seems to happen only when social consciousness reaches a level where interaction with outside peoples has to be taken into the tribe's consideration." Thus, once societies became aware of other people outside their own society ("them" instead of just "us"), they began to design cities that emphasized their insider status. "Peoples in this stage . . . often used their very city plans as aggressive instruments for extending power. They simply pushed their ordered streets outward to include and enclose neighboring tribes."

The Grid Pattern

An orthogonal, or perpendicular, grid pattern of streets and buildings was another feature of cities designed by societies that wished to demonstrate their keen sense of order. In the fourth century B.C., Alexander the Great championed the grid as the trademark of

Greek civilization. The city the Greek conqueror designed for himself in Egypt, called Alexandria, made liberal use of the grid pattern. Interestingly, it was in Alexandria that the most well known cartographer of all time, Claudius Ptolemy, worked and studied centuries later. Ptolemy's own use of the grid pattern was to become an important element of mapmaking.

Like the Greeks and the Romans after them, the ancient Chinese used the grid pattern to organize their cities. According to Edgerton, the Chinese also began using grids as mapping tools around the time that Alexandrian scholars began using them. However, the Chinese only saw the grid as a scale of fixed distances, a way of measuring units of land in relation to one another, for example. They did not try to relate the grid's proportions to the entire earth's size, the way modern cartographers do. When the Greeks began to relate their map grids to the sun's passage over the earth, and later to their idea of the earth's size based on astronomic calculations rather than myth, a great breakthrough in cartography had been achieved in Western civilization.

Connecting Earth and Universe

Before ancient Greek thinkers could make progress toward an accurate world map, they had to agree on the earth's shape. According to Pythagoras, a pupil of Anaximander in the sixth century B.C., the sphere was perfect, the ideal form. Therefore, the earth must be round. The idea of the earth being a perfect shape appealed to the Greek mind. But no one could figure out how to see the earth's shape when people were confined to the earth's surface.

Two centuries later, the great thinker Aristotle thought he had enough evidence to endorse Pythagoras's theory

Alexander the Great chose the grid pattern when he planned the city of Alexandria in the fourth century B.C.

cal world, a world that included the possibility of other people in far-off places.

The Size of the World

But who were these people, and just how far away were they? Eratosthenes did much to answer the second question. An important figure in the history of cartography, Eratosthenes worked at the Royal Library in Alexandria in the third century B.C. He made the first accurate measurement of the earth's circumference, or the distance around the earth's surface. To do so, he used a gnomon, a simple device thought to have been invented by Anaximander of Miletus. It was a straight rod held vertically to cast a shadow. The shadow's length was used to calculate latitude, or one's position on earth relative to the equator. People used gnomons to figure the angle at which the sun's rays slanted

The Greek thinker Aristotle endorsed Pythagoras's theory that the earth was a sphere and gathered evidence to prove it.

that the earth was round. He noticed that the shadow of the earth cast on the moon during a lunar eclipse is always round. He also observed that ships disappearing over the horizon always disappear as if dipping over a curved surface. Travelers, who by this time had started to venture farther afield, reported that the farther north or south one traveled, the lower in the sky certain constellations appeared to sink. Thus, thousands of years before their suspicions could be confirmed by a trip on a space shuttle, the Greeks let go of their disklike earth to embrace a spheri-

Eratosthenes used a gnomon to make the first accurate measurement of the circumference of the earth in the third century B.C.

down on a particular spot on the earth. The gnomon was also used as a sundial.

According to Berthon and Robinson, there were three steps to Eratosthenes' calculation of the earth's size. First, he needed to find a place where the sun stood directly overhead at midday. It was reported that in the city of Syene, on the summer solstice (June 21) each year, the sun was directly overhead at noon. Second, he needed to pinpoint the distance between Syene and Alexandria. He calculated this by determining the number of days it took a camel caravan traveling at a certain speed to make the journey between the two places. Third, he measured, by gnomon, the angle of the sun's rays in Alexandria at the same time and date. The angle, 7 degrees, was about a fiftieth of a circle. (The Babylonians had al-ready developed the system of dividing a circle into 360 degrees.) To find the earth's circumference, itself a circle, Eratosthenes then multiplied the distance between the two cities by 50. Amazingly, his result was within 200 miles of the true figure of 24,862 miles.

The Latitude and Longitude Grid

About one hundred years later, another revolutionary thinker who had a lasting influence on cartography surfaced, the astronomer Hipparchus of Rhodes. He imagined that the globe was divided lengthwise and breadthwise into 360 degrees, forming an invisible grid of latitude and longitude lines, also known as parallels and meridians. This system

This map from the third century B.C. depicts the world according to Eratosthenes.

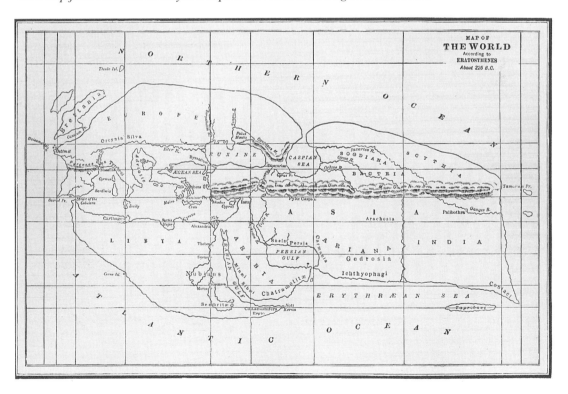

Third-century astronomer Hipparchus theorized that the globe of the earth could be divided lengthwise and breadthwise into 360 degrees, forming latitudinal and longitudinal lines.

said than done in ancient times. Latitude could be measured by means of the gnomon, like the one that Eratosthenes used to measure the angle of the sun in Alexandria. But, as Berthon and Robinson point out, gnomons were not easy for travelers to carry in their pockets. Some were as long as thirty-five feet. Longitude was much harder for the ancients to calculate because it involved comparing the time of day in which a global event, such as an eclipse, occurred at widely separated locations. The problem of determining longitude persisted for centuries.

Eratosthenes' estimate of the earth's size and Hipparchus's idea of applying a regularly spaced grid to the globe based on precise astronomical calculation made the Greek world map more than just a symbol of humanity's place in the universe. It gave maps the potential to become precise tools for exploring. They no longer simply gave people a comforting, if mythic, sense of where they were. They could also point out where people might go, and ultimately, exactly how long it would take and precisely in what direction to head.

Although the Greeks understood the exciting possibilities of the grid concept, they were far from acting on its potential. Because travel was hindered by their level of technological development, much of the world remained hidden from them. By the second century B.C., they had just begun to realize how much there was yet to know. The circular world had opened outward. What lay beyond the horizon was still a mystery, an ocean of darkness.

would allow an individual to discover the distance as well as the direction between any two places on earth. To use the grid an observer had to locate his or her own latitude between the poles as well as his or her longitude between east and west. If the observer could achieve this, he or she could tell how far away and in what direction he or she was from any other point on the grid.

However, for a long time Hipparchus's grid remained only a theory, because locating one's precise latitude and longitude coordinates was easier

CHAPTER 2

One Step Forward, Two Steps Back

Four centuries after Eratosthenes worked there, the Royal Library at Alexandria hosted another important scientist, Claudius Ptolemy. His work influenced cartography for the next fourteen centuries. Ptolemy, who lived from about A.D. 100 to 170, was a Greek mathematician, astronomer, and geographer. Among other books, he wrote a famous guide to mapmaking called the *Geography*. He based his ideas about maps on the work of others, as well as on his own research. According to Samuel Y. Edgerton Jr., "Ptolemy's system represented

the summation of the Alexandrian school of Greek cartography."

A Guide to Mapping

Ptolemy's *Geography* was an eight-volume guide to mapping the earth. It contained more than two dozen detailed maps of different parts of the world. These maps corresponded to a larger map of the earth, laid out according to a latitude and longitude grid that Ptolemy based on mathematical calculations and astronomical data. The prime meridian (zero degrees longitude) passed through the Canary Islands. Ptolemy's world extended 180 degrees eastward to China.

The *Geography* was truly the first how-to book for mapmakers. In the first volume, Ptolemy discussed cartography in general, then described his mapmaking methods in detail. A reader could use the methods he described to put together a map by checking Ptolemy's latitude and longitude tables. These tables, listing Ptolemy's coordinates for some eight thousand place names, made up volumes two through eight of the *Geography*.

Ptolemy drew much of his information from another geographer, Marinus of Tyre. But, unlike other geographers' chatty discussions of people and places, Ptolemy stuck to mathematics. He did not want to tell entertaining travel stories. He wanted to create a system for

First-century scientist Claudius Ptolemy wrote an eight-volume guide to mapmaking called Geography. *It contained more than two dozen maps of different parts of the world.*

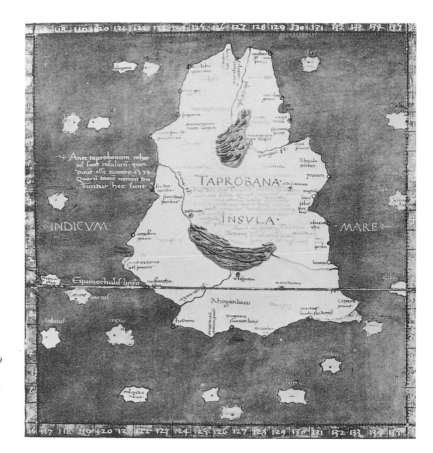

Two pages from Ptolemy's Geography. Although Ptolemy attempted to forge an accurate map of the known world, he had to gather his information from reports of travelers who often exaggerated and embellished their adventures.

putting the known world down on record as accurately as possible.

Not much is known about Ptolemy. Writers either praise him for his originality or criticize him for keeping alive the errors of his fellow scholars. According to Lloyd A. Brown:

> His original contributions to science may have been few, as some writers suggest, but he was never guilty of plagiarism. He improved much of what he copied and developed the ideas he borrowed. He repeated many of the important theories of his predecessors, but stated them better and more clearly. He usually gave credit where credit was due.

However, Simon Berthon and Andrew Robinson picture Ptolemy

sitting in the candle-lit corners of Alexandria's great library, hunched over his quill and parchment rolls, a [fussy] man who copied his predecessors calculations while delighting in pointing out . . . their errors.

Berthon and Robinson are surprised that Ptolemy would warn mapmakers about the inaccuracy of travelers' tales, and then end up accepting wrong information himself.

Ptolemy's position must have been frustrating. According to Brown, the scientist admitted that people knew many details about some parts of the earth, but next to nothing about other parts. Many of his estimates of distance and direction depended on unscientifically measured, unverified travelers' reports. Travelers tended to brag, magnifying the length of their journeys. They gave disappointingly general descriptions of distance and direction: "A few days' voyage," "an overland march of four months," "towards the summer sunrise," "towards Africa." Although he was a stickler for accuracy, Ptolemy had to settle for whatever information he could get and, as Brown puts it, "dream of the time when travelers would take careful notes and astronomers could get around to different places and find out the truth about things."

The Astrolabe

Ptolemy believed serious mapmakers should double-check all guesswork about the location of places and the distances between them by using gnomons and astrolabes. An astrolabe was a round

An astrolabe was used by ancient astronomers to measure the angle of a star's elevation. Believing it to be more accurate than the gnomon, Ptolemy urged all astronomers to double-check their calculations by using the astrolabe.

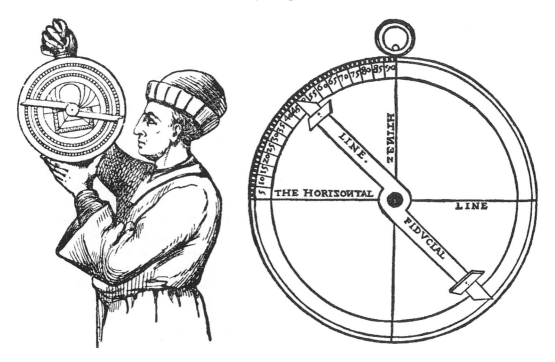

piece of flat metal or wood whose rim was divided into 360 degrees. A straight arm rotated from the hub of this wheel. The arm could be lined up with a star to measure its angle of elevation. A tool used by Ptolemy, the astrolabe was more accurate than a gnomon, and it was more convenient. It did not depend on the sun casting a shadow, so it could make use of features of the night sky.

Ptolemy recognized the need to pinpoint the earth's correct size and shape. If a mapmaker took mathematical measurements of the earth with devices such as astrolabes, then he or she could accurately show the earth's features in relationship to one another, without distorting land masses or misplacing cities. According to Brown,

Ptolemy believed the cartographer's mission was

> to survey the whole of the world "in its just proportions," that is, to scale. He likened the problem to that of the painter who must first work out the outline of a figure in correct proportion before he fills in the minute details of feature and form.

Ptolemy's Errors

Despite his concern for precision, Ptolemy made major errors in constructing his world map. His biggest mistake was deciding to reject Eratosthenes' figure for the earth's circumference and replace it with a figure used by Marinus of Tyre. This measurement was nearly

This map shows Ptolemy's major innovation, that of representing a round globe on a flat map, or projection. Ptolemy also started the tradition of setting up a map so that north is at the top and east is at the right.

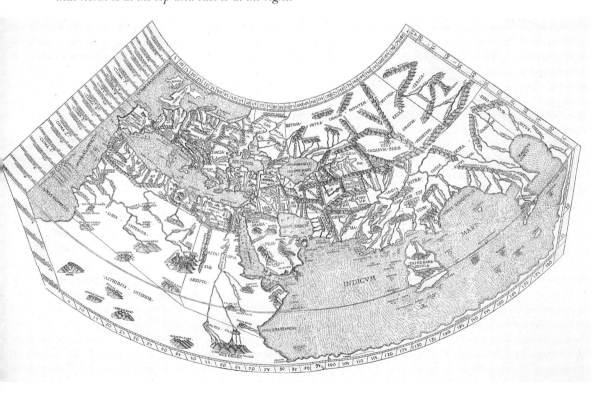

one-third too small. The error persisted for centuries. In addition, Ptolemy drew his equator about four hundred miles too far north, and his latitude and longitude tables were based on incorrect information. These errors slowed the progress of cartography after him as much as his innovations helped it.

Map Projection

Ptolemy's major innovation was representing a round globe on a flat map, a method called projection. In his *Geography*, he wrote that there are two ways of making a portrait of the world: reproduce it on a sphere, or draw it on a flat surface. But a globe large enough to show everything in detail would be too large to see at a glance. As Berthon and Robinson explain:

> By Ptolemy's time the inhabited world was becoming too large and knowledge of its contents too detailed to allow easy display on the restricted size of a globe. . . . But how could the curved meridians and parallels be projected onto a flat piece of parchment?

Cartographers before Ptolemy had simply used a grid of straight lines intersecting at right angles. But as Berthon and Robinson point out:

> This would have worked perfectly for a flat Earth, even for a small area of our round Earth where the curvature of its surface was insignificant. Used over the whole world, however, the grid led to extreme distortions. The solution was to draw some lines as curves.

Ptolemy gave detailed instructions to mapmakers about how to achieve different types of map projection.

Ptolemy also believed in dividing the world map into continents, regions, or towns. These segments could be drawn to large or small scale. Why do this? In a map of the entire earth, the early mapmakers tended to sacrifice proportion, or scale, to squeeze everything onto the map. Mapmakers also tended to exaggerate the size of well-known areas to accommodate every detail and to shrink the size of lesser-known areas. Dividing up the world map would make it easier to read and would protect the accuracy of the picture. For practical reasons, Ptolemy also started the tradition that we use today of setting up a map so that north is at the top and east is at the right. He did this because, in his day, the world's better-known areas were clustered in the northeast. On a flat map, Ptolemy believed, it was easier to study places positioned in the upper right corner.

Terra Incognita

Ptolemy's world map included an unknown land, or terra incognita. When Ptolemy imagined the known world on a globe, he felt the need to add an unknown land to balance lands he knew. According to Edgerton, Ptolemy's map projections suggested that his meridians and parallels continued to curve around the known half of the globe to enclose a terra incognita beyond it. This mysterious land could be mapped in the same way the inhabited world had been. Before it had even been discovered, then, the unknown territory had been tied to the rest of the world by means of the cartographic grid. According to Brown:

> [Ptolemy] abandoned the idea of a world encompassed by water. . . . Instead, he recognized the possibility and probability of Terra Incognita beyond

the limits of his arbitrary boundary lines. In other words, he left the matter open to further investigation. This attitude was an important step in the progress of cartography and an incentive to further exploration.

Ptolemy's world map implied that the unknown land might someday become known.

A Divine Viewpoint

Ptolemy's world map was not only important to exploration and to cartography, but to society, according to Edgerton. It carried on the ancient tradition of mapping as a way of linking societies to heaven, because the way it was constructed satisfied "that innate human desire to have the visual image of this world organized according to some higher universal ordering system." But in Ptolemy's worldview, the observer could imagine viewing the world from the sky, as if looking at it from the point of view of the gods themselves, with the gods' own insight into the natural order of the universe.

Ptolemy dreamed of an orderly mapping of the world according to a scientific system. He did not succeed in designing an accurate world map in his lifetime, but his vision was an inspiration to those who came after him, including Christopher Columbus, who, Brown wrote, "pinned his hopes on Ptolemy and discovered a world—by accident." But before Ptolemy's *Geography* became a force of change during the Renaissance, it would be lost to Europe for centuries after the rise of Christianity in the Middle Ages.

During the Middle Ages, beginning around A.D. 300 and lasting until almost 1500, Christian thought dominated in Europe, at cartography's expense. People worried about their route to the afterlife; they did not care about mapping the physical world, only the spiritual world. Islamic cartographers continued to progress, but in the Christian world symbolic maps replaced Ptolemy's careful grids and astronomic calculations.

Lloyd A. Brown explains the attitude of Christians toward scientific study during this period:

> Much of the intellectual twilight of the early Middle Ages, beginning in 300 A.D., was caused by nothing more than man's preoccupation with his newfound road to glory and the sublime prospect of the hereafter. . . . Human experience, close observation of natural phenomena, no longer mattered.

During the Middle Ages, Christians sacrificed map accuracy to their beliefs by placing the center of Christianity, Jerusalem, at the center of their maps, as depicted in this manuscript from 1275.

Early Christians believed geography should match biblical theory. This thirteenth-century world map, owned by Hereford Cathedral in England, shows Christ overlooking the world.

The early Christians preferred a symbolic representation of the world, with Christianity as its theme. Literal maps of the world were counterproductive to the aim of religion, they thought. Progress made with scientific methods for cartography was suppressed in the Christian world for centuries. According to Brown:

> At the beginning of the Christian era, and for the next twelve hundred years or so, only the brave and the pagan indulged in geographic speculation. It was impious if not downright sinful to probe the mysteries of the universe. . . . Maps were made furtively, studied secretly, and in many cases destroyed promptly.

Early Christian Maps

The early Christians looked to the Bible to decide how they should draw their maps. According to writer William E. Phipps, one of the earliest Christian mapmakers was a Byzantine monk named Cosmas, who lived in the sixth century A.D. He believed that a true map must follow scriptural guidelines. Cosmas drew a rectangular world map, because he interpreted the eighth chapter of Hebrews to mean that the earth was a rectangle like Moses' tabernacle.

In the seventh century A.D., according to Phipps, a Spanish bishop named Isidore of Seville was inspired to draw a

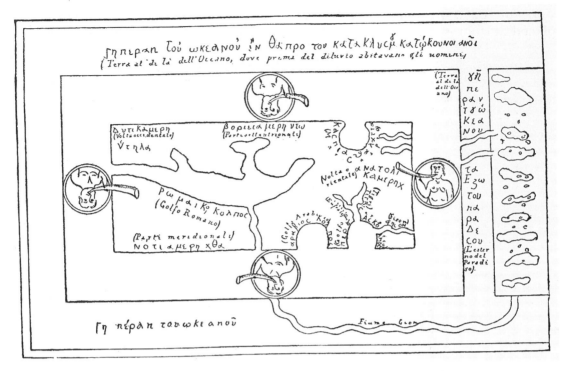

A rectangular world map produced by the Byzantine monk Cosmas, who lived in the sixth century. Cosmas chose a rectangle to match Moses' tabernacle.

circular world map after reading Ezekiel 5:5. Isidore placed Jerusalem in the center of his circular map because Ezekiel says, "This is Jerusalem; I have set her in the center of the nations."

T-O Maps

The T-O map was the most popular world map of the Middle Ages. Like the ancients' maps of a disk-shaped earth surrounded by water, this map form demonstrated that its Christian makers were under the spell of the omphalos syndrome. They believed that Christianity, represented by the holy city of Jerusalem, was at the center of the world. The T-O world map shows Jerusalem in the middle, surrounded by the three continents of Asia, Europe,

and Africa. The ocean surrounds everything, forming the circular O of the T-O map. The T portion is made up of the rivers and seas that separate the three continents. This T shape crosses at Jerusalem.

The T-O map was popular because it echoed Christian scripture. The central location of Jerusalem was based on firm Christian belief. In the same way, the splitting of the world's surface into three continents, an idea that was originated by the Greeks and Romans, was continued. The arrangement agreed with the story in Genesis that the earth was divided after the great flood among Noah's three sons, Shem, Ham, and Japheth. On the T-O map, Shem is represented by Asia, Ham is Africa, and Japheth is Europe. Even the way the map was turned reflected Christian thought. East, instead of north, was placed at the top because east was the symbolic direction of paradise.

Although the T-O map was a satisfying picture of the Christian world for the early Christians who viewed it, it raised some disturbing questions. If Jerusalem was the center of the Christian world, then the Europeans were outsiders, living near the Holy Land, but not in it. According to Edgerton:

> The T-O map was a matter of considerable embarrassment to the Christian pope, who could not, like his counterparts in China and Islam, put his finger on the center and say smugly, "There sit I at the shrine of our faith, in the midst of fellow believers."

The T-O map may even have been responsible for early Christian crusading, or missionary journeys, Phipps observes:

> These highly subjective T and O representations of reality probably encouraged European Christians to join

crusades which aimed at recapturing the center of the world from the "infidels." It was humiliating for Western Europeans to feel as though they lived at the [outside edge] of lands God gave to the faithful.

Thus, even a symbolic map could inspire exploration and conquest.

The Ebstorf World Map

The Ebstorf world map is an extreme example of the unique way Christians saw their world. Created around 1235, it was a large chart about eleven feet square, named after the German monastery where it was discovered. It was later destroyed in the bombing of Hanover during World War II, but color photographs of it survive. Like a T-O map, the Ebstorf world map displays Jerusalem in the middle, and it is turned so that east is at the top. The unusual thing about the map is that the image of Jesus' body is superimposed

Isidore of Seville was the first to draw the T-O map, a circular map with Jerusalem at the center (left). The diagram on the right explains the symbolism of the T-O map.

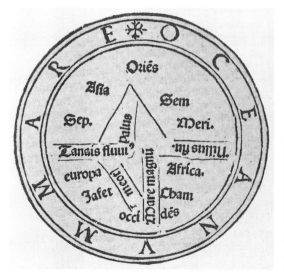

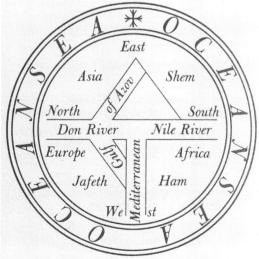

over it. Christ's head is drawn in detail at the top of the map. Rivers running through the continents represent his veins. Jesus' pierced hands at the left and right touch the north and south edges of the world.

On the Ebstorf world map, the feet of Jesus appear at the bottom, at the Pillars of Hercules, the two high rocks at the east end of the Strait of Gibraltar between Europe and Africa. The Pillars of Hercules marked the farthest limit of the known world in the Middle Ages. (The classical Greeks had pushed the western edge of their known world farther out, making it the Canary Islands, where Ptolemy had drawn his prime meridian, but the early Christians had reverted back to the earlier landmark.) Edgerton describes the unique arrangement this way:

> Christ's feet are at Gibraltar, the bottom and the western exit from the Mediterranean. Here the legendary Hercules is supposed to have erected two pillars with the inscription, *Non plus ultra*. "There is nothing beyond." Jerusalem is the Savior's sacred umbilicus.

This famous thirteenth century map literally shows the world as equal to the body of Christ. Viewers would not be faithful Christians if they considered the existence of a world beyond its borders. As Edgerton puts it:

> Nor could the Good Christian think seriously of sailing away through the Pillars of Hercules, because that . . . would mean abandoning the Body of Christ. Certainly, here is an important reason why medieval Christians were loath to adventure westward across the Ocean before Columbus.

Thus, a map could influence a society's worldview, appealing to its religious loyalty as well as to its superstitions, in ways that would remain influential for centuries to come.

Medieval Islamic Maps

While Europe slumbered, Islam made great strides in cartography. After the death of the Moslem prophet Mohammed in A.D. 632, the religion of Islam swept through Mesopotamia, Palestine, Egypt, North Africa, and parts of Spain. The Moslems craved new learning. Among the classical thinkers they studied were Aristotle for philosophy, Galen for medicine, and Ptolemy for geography and astronomy.

Islam's classical thinkers studied Aristotle, Galen (pictured), and Ptolemy in their quest for knowledge.

The Moslem prophet Mohammed founded the religion of Islam. Islam's followers made great strides in cartography.

Edgerton points out that Ptolemy's worldview served the Mohammedans well:

> Not only had [Ptolemy] inadvertently blessed Mecca as the "navel of the world" by its [nearness] to the . . . astronomically determined center of his original [world map], but the longitude/latitude system would make it possible for the most far-flung faithful of Islam to know precisely in which direction to bow.

Thus, the Moslems were using maps to support their religious beliefs in the Middle East at the same time Christians were doing the same thing in western Europe.

For about three hundred years, Moslem scholars read Ptolemy in the original Greek. After the fall of Babylon in southwest Asia in the ninth century, the Moslem caliph founded an academy for learning in Baghdad called the Hagia Sophia (Greek for "sacred wisdom"). There, the major Greek works, including Ptolemy's, were translated into Arabic.

As knowledge of Ptolemy became available to the Arabs, the development of Islamic cartography continued to progress. Increasingly, Moslems used astronomical calculations to determine the latitude and longitude of places on earth. As they became better at it, they improved Ptolemy's estimates. For example, Islamic mapmakers reduced the length of the Mediterranean Sea, given by Ptolemy as 62 degrees, to the correct figure of 42 degrees. Moslems also began making extensive land and sea journeys for trading, government business, or to conquer other settlements. The geographical descriptions reported by Islamic travelers were taken into account on detailed route maps designed to make travel easier.

Al-Idrisi

Al-Idrisi, who lived from 1099 to 1166, was one such traveler. He was also one of Islam's most respected cartographers. Al-Idrisi was familiar with Christianity's circular T-O maps from his European journeys. But he had his own ideas about what a world map should look like. His maps were just as influenced by his beliefs as the Christians' maps were. According to William E. Phipps:

> Idrisi reoriented the widespread Christian map so as to give Islam the propaganda advantage. Christendom is demoted to the bottom of the map and the dark skinned people are at the top.

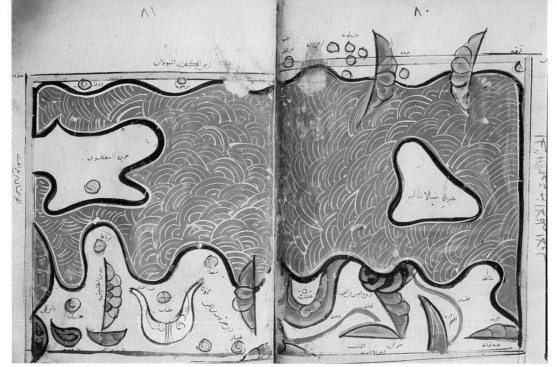

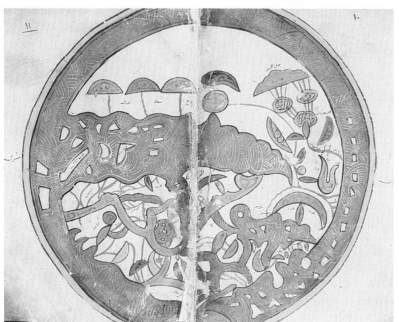

Although Al-Idrisi's map depicted the world differently from the Christian T-O maps, it still reflected the mapmaker's worldview. Al-Idrisi placed the Christian nations at the bottom. Two of his maps are pictured here— India is represented above, while Egypt, surrounded by the Mediterranean, is pictured below.

Africa—Idrisi's home continent—is larger than all the other land areas combined.

Thus, whether Christian or Moslem, religion often directed the shapes medieval maps took. After twelve centuries of fascination with religious ways of seeing the world, European civilization was ready to turn its eyes back to the practical, physical world and begin to explore it systematically, with maps as guides. The rediscovery of Ptolemy's *Geography* in Europe had much to do with that reawakening.

CHAPTER 3

Charting the Course

Before interest in Ptolemy's *Geography* returned in the early fifteenth century, western Europe had already begun using a revolutionary new kind of map called the portolan chart. These detailed maps of coastlines became popular tools for sailors by the end of the twelfth century, appearing in the Mediterranean area around the same time as the mariner's compass. The precise charts were based on descriptions of the Mediterranean and Black Seas and their coastlines as reported by sailors who knew the waters well. They showed main ports and coastal features. This helped seafarers plan their voyages and stay on course. Portolan charts were beautifully outlined by hand on sheepskin. Straight lines crisscrossed the charts, marking the thirty-two directions of the mariner's compass.

These surprisingly accurate sea charts were thought to originate in Genoa, in northern Italy, and their significance was far reaching. They were storehouses of information important to trade and politics as well as to cartography. According to G.R. Crone in *Maps and Their Makers:*

> Their history is a good instance of the response of technicians to a new social demand, in this case the need of the commercial communities of Italy to develop communications with their

This painting of fourteenth-century Venice depicts the importance of trading and sailing and, by extension, accurate maps to the Renaissance world.

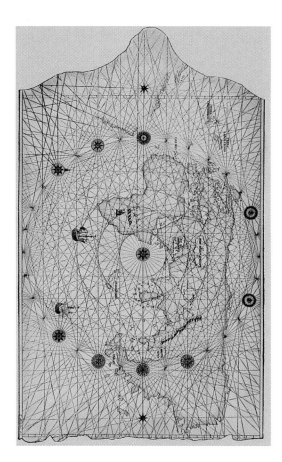

Portolan charts such as this one from 1502 contained crucial navigating information and were highly valued by seafaring nations.

[Portolan charts] were much more than an aid to navigation; they were, in effect, the key to empire, the way to wealth. As such, their development in the early stages was shrouded in mystery, for the way to wealth is seldom shared.

Portolan charts heralded Christian Europe's new interest in the world's actual appearance. The sea charts came into use about the same time that Christians had begun to grow dissatisfied with their symbolic, religion-based methods of mapping. According to Samuel Y. Edgerton Jr.:

> Discouraged by their failure to recapture the Holy Land, medieval Christians had begun to lose faith in . . . their visual and pictorial conventions. By the thirteenth century . . . they were demanding a new set of such conventions so that they might better "see" the world, quantitatively this time rather than mystically.

Christians of the late Middle Ages still had faith in heaven, but they also yearned for facts about earth, outlined precisely on realistic maps.

The Rediscovery of Ptolemy

A little more than one hundred years after portolan charts were introduced, Europe got another chance to develop more accurate maps with the rediscovery of Ptolemy's writings. In the fourteenth century, Turkey invaded Byzantium. Refugees fled, packing treasures with them, including the Greek texts of Ptolemy's works. The smuggled manuscripts made it to Florence, Italy. Geography and mathematics were becoming important studies in this cosmopolitan city. By 1410, Ptolemy had

expanding markets. The achievement of these thirteenth-century cartographers was a notable contribution to knowledge, and one which was not surpassed for centuries.

Portolan charts became important records of sailors' discoveries as their voyages got longer and riskier in response to the demands of trade. Because they contained crucial navigating information, they were valuable documents. In fact, Spain and Portugal soon decided to declare their portolan charts state secrets—slipping them to rival nations was punishable by death. Lloyd A. Brown explains:

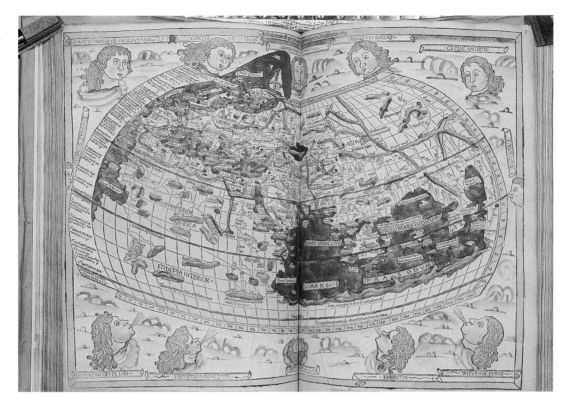

Ptolemy's grid pattern, dormant throughout the Middle Ages, became popular again during the Renaissance.

been translated into Latin. Copies of the translated *Geography*, first without and later with the accompanying maps, fell into the hands of European scholars, who enthusiastically welcomed the ideas contained in them.

Europe Embraces Ptolemy

Even the artist Leonardo da Vinci, one of the great thinkers of the Renaissance, owned a copy of Ptolemy's work and mentioned it frequently in his many notebooks. What intrigued da Vinci about Ptolemy? According to Edgerton:

> It was hardly Ptolemy's geographical information as such that interested Leonardo. Much of that was wrong or obsolete anyway. Rather it was the organizing system of the atlas by which Ptolemy coordinated his pictures of the individual lands with their relative positions into the [world map]. This depended on imagining the globe . . . as a . . . surface ruled by a uniform geometric grid. Here was the true essence of the world, thought Leonardo, not its wrinkled coastlines and willy-nilly mountains and plains.

Once again, the idea of the grid had caught the public imagination.

Ptolemy's famous grid influenced both art and politics during the Renaissance, Edgerton points out. In Masaccio's painting *Trinity* (about 1425) the artist creates the illusion of curved surfaces, just as a projected map does. The

During the Renaissance, Ptolemy's grid pattern could be found in art, sculpture, and even architecture. The ceiling of Masaccio's Trinity *is adorned with the vastly popular pattern.*

cartographic grid inspired not only artists. Powerful religious leaders were also interested. Pope Pius II became a fan of Ptolemy. In the 1460s, he wrote a long report on the *Geography*, praising Ptolemy's longitude/latitude system. He even had a gridded world map built in his palace garden.

Because the new grid system suggested a way to organize and order any part of the globe, it began to stand for a way Christian Europe could spread itself across the world. As Edgerton puts it, "The new grid cartography, especially in the hands of the Roman popes, tended to reinforce faith in the divine mission of Christianity to convert the

world. . . . The cartographic grid in the Renaissance was believed to exude moral power."

Ptolemy's ideas had great scientific impact, as well as social influence. Cartographers of the Renaissance were impressed most by two features of Ptolemy's *Geography*: 1) projecting the curved earth accurately on a flat surface, and 2) the idea of representing any point on earth as two intersecting lines—the grid system of longitude and latitude.

The Printing Press Fuels the Age of Exploration

Ptolemy's rediscovery in Europe marked one of three major events of the fifteenth century. The other two events related to the first: the printing press was introduced in Europe, and Columbus reached the New World.

Surprisingly, Ptolemy's world map was not the first map to be printed on the new printing presses. According to William E. Phipps, the first map printed in Augsburg, Germany, in 1472 was St. Isidore's T-O map. That map would soon fade from popularity as multiple copies of Ptolemy's *Geography* began to fly from the presses. Christopher Columbus, a sailor from Genoa, Italy, was one of Ptolemy's many readers.

A Florentine thinker named Paolo dal Pozzo Toscanelli was also familiar with the possibilities of Ptolemy's grid and the promise it offered to sailors eager to go where no one in Europe had been before. He began writing letters to Christopher Columbus. Toscanelli told him that if he sailed beyond the Pillars of Hercules (at the western end of the Mediterranean Sea), he would find a western sea route to the East. According to Edgerton, "Toscanelli even sent Columbus a gridded map (unfortunately now lost) of the ocean sea in order to make his point more graphically. Columbus, thoroughly convinced, went off to sell the idea to the Spanish." Thus, many centuries later, Ptolemy's work inspired Columbus's discovery, not of Asia, but of a new continent, America.

The age of exploration, beginning with Columbus in 1492, moved ahead rapidly. By the mid-sixteenth century, crowds of explorers had rushed to the New World. After so many centuries of standing guard, the fabled Pillars of Hercules held no power to trap western European ships within the boundaries of the Mediterranean. There were farther shores Europe hungered to claim.

Philosopher Paolo dal Pozza Toscanelli convinced Christopher Columbus (above) that he could find a western sea route to the east by sailing past the Pillars of Hercules. Although the map Toscanelli sent Columbus was lost, other Toscanelli maps survive. An example of one Toscanelli map appears below.

Tools of the Navigator

The exploration explosion intensified the need for tools to create accurate charts. When navigators headed for distant shores, they needed to know how to avoid hidden reefs and rocks that could wreck their ships. Navigators needed to be able to estimate how long it would take before the ship docked at its final port so that enough supplies could be stored on board. And, according to Brown, a navigator needed to know which way to steer the ship: "Arriving late at a destination may be inconvenient or even hazardous, but without an accurate knowledge of direction, a navigator will never arrive at all."

Ferdinand and Isabella ponder Columbus's map, which he used to convince the monarchs that he could accomplish his bold plan of reaching the Indies via a western sea route.

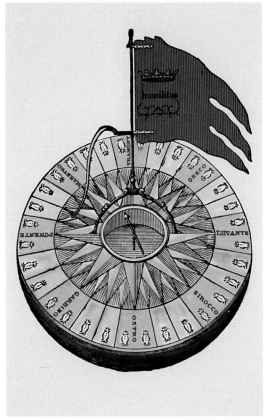

Even with the mariner's compass (above) methods for charting sailing routes were primitive.

Methods for charting courses varied from the technical to the casual. According to writer Peter Ryan, "South till the butter melts, and then due west," was one of the recommendations given by early navigators trying to sail to America. Ryan does not mention whether the crew ever made it there. This hit-or-miss method of travel planning, used by sailors who relied on experience and just plain guesswork, was called dead reckoning.

However, it was tough to obtain precise readings of distance and direction at sea. Buffeting winds made it impossible to go in a straight line, so it was hard to get a sense of how far a ship had voyaged. The mariner's compass, which had arrived in the Mediterranean region about three hundred years earlier, was still the most advanced navigating tool in use. (In China, compasses had been used on land by the fifth century A.D., and by the eleventh century at sea, about one hundred years before their arrival in Europe.) The magnetic instrument was steeped in superstition. Compasses were rumored to have the power to bring quarreling wives and husbands back together, a comforting thought to sailors who were often away at sea.

Even with the help of the compass, methods for charting courses remained primitive. One way sailors estimated their ships' speed (knowing this helped them calculate distance) was to throw a log overboard at the front of the boat and measure, by means of a sandglass, how long it took the log to bob up in the churning waters behind the boat. This inconvenient routine is said to have inspired the phrase "ship's log." Mariners could also consult lists called "traverse tables" worked out in advance to help plan their routes. The combination of portolan chart, traverse table, and compass, plus a lot of lucky dead reckoning, saved most ships from veering off course in nearby waters. Familiar routes were already fairly well charted. The uncharted Atlantic posed the big challenge to seafarers.

The Longitude Puzzle

Renaissance navigators knew that the key to charting an accurate course was longitude. But how to determine longitude remained a thorny problem. To know one's exact position on the net-

British clock maker John Harrison solved the problem of finding longitude at sea in 1762 when he invented his remarkably accurate Number 4 chronometer.

work of latitude and longitude lines encircling the earth, one needed to know the earth's size. The distance between degrees of longitude had to be based on that size. Cartographers were still unsure of the size of the earth, and Ptolemy's impression that it was smaller than it actually is had not helped matters. Furthermore, mathematics was still in its infancy at the beginning of the Renaissance, and clocks—still early in their development—ran too fast or slow to be used in calculations. It would not be until the eighteenth century that the problem of finding longitude at sea in the absence of landmarks would be solved, when British clock maker John Harrison invented his Number 4 chronometer in 1762. Until then, sailors could not put their understanding of the cartographic grid to full practical use.

LATITUDE AND LONGITUDE

The ability to locate a point anywhere on earth began with an idea introduced by the second-century Greek astronomer Hipparchus. Hipparchus imagined a grid of crosswise lines dividing the globe. These are the lines of latitude and longitude.

Latitude describes a north or south position in relation to the equator. All points on the equator have a latitude of zero degrees. The North Pole has a latitude of 90 degrees north and all points between the equator and the North Pole lie in the northern latitudes. The South Pole has a latitude of 90 degrees south and all points between the equator and the South Pole lie in the southern latitudes.

Longitude describes the east or west position of a point on the earth's surface in relation to an imaginary line called the Prime Meridian. Like the Prime Meridian, which runs through Greenwich, England, the lines of longitude run north and south along the earth's surface. Most countries have agreed that Greenwich lies at zero degrees longitude.

The latitude-longitude grid could not be put to practical use during Hipparchus's time. The tools for measuring latitude existed, but the tools for finding longitude did not. Once those tools were developed, many centuries later, one could pinpoint any location on earth.

The First Scientifically Based Maps

The Renaissance's age of exploration marked a giant leap in cartography's development. According to writer Juergen Schulz:

> Between the first Portuguese voyages along the west coast of Africa in the 1430s, and the rounding of Cape Horn in 1616, innumerable new lands were discovered and there was a surge in the quality and quantity of map production. The output of printed maps leapt from a handful to hundreds per year. By the end of the sixteenth century the interest in maps had spread to the educated public.

The renewed popularity of Ptolemy's theories, the development of portolan charts, the discoveries of explorers, and the refinement of practical scientific instruments like the compass combined to improve the quality of Renaissance maps. But these maps still reflected the

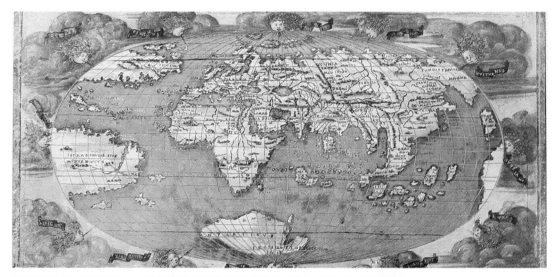

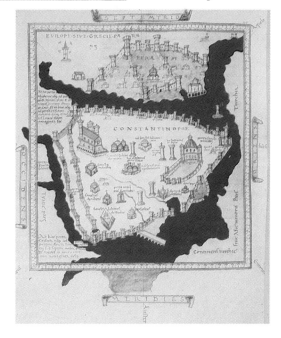

Cartography's development can be traced in these maps from the sixteenth century. (Top) A world map by Francesco Rosselli in 1508; (middle) another map of the world from 1502; (bottom) a mariner's chart showing Constantinople.

limits of the knowledge available to mapmakers, such as ways to determine latitude and longitude correctly.

Mercator's Projection

Nevertheless, many small steps since the European rediscovery of Ptolemy made possible a famous forerunner of modern maps. In 1538, a mapmaker named Gerhardus Mercator from Flanders (in northern Belgium) published the first world map that included North and South America. But his most noteworthy achievement proved to be his new method of map projection developed in 1569. Projection had become especially

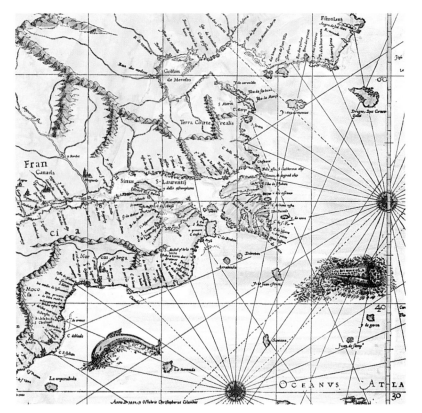

Maps changed dramatically in 1569 because of Gerhardus Mercator (below). Mercator widened the space between latitude lines the farther south or north they were drawn to compensate for the circumference of the earth. A portion of a Mercator map, dated 1569, appears at left.

vital to navigators. Sailors crossed the curved surface of the ocean, but they needed map grids made up of straight lines to set their compass courses between points with ease. On maps representing large areas, the mapmaker who wanted to keep grid lines straight for navigators needed to adjust somehow for the earth's roundness. Mercator decided to solve the problem by widening the space between latitude lines the farther south or north they were drawn.

Mercator's map projection turned out to be a big help to navigators charting their courses. It was so popular that it became the standard format for world maps for four hundred years, well into the twentieth century. However, it also had a major flaw: It twisted continents and seas out of shape for the person looking at the map. Lands near the

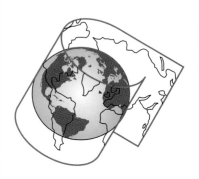

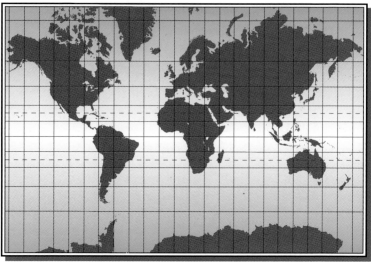

A

B

Mercator's projection introduced a new way of showing the round earth on a flat sheet of paper. The round earth can be thought of as a balloon covered with crisscross parallels and meridians. Such a balloon can be placed inside a cylinder with its middle (the equator) just touching the cylinder's walls (A). If the balloon is inflated, as it expands the curved meridians will straighten and flatten against the cylinder walls. Each parallel, one after the other, will push against the cylinder, but the top and bottom of the balloon (the earth's polar caps) will never quite be able to touch the cylinder walls. If the cylinder is unrolled and flattened, the imprint transferred onto it by the balloon is a cylindrical projection (B).

equator, such as India, look smaller than they really are. Lands near the north and south poles, such as Greenland, are stretched much too large. This distortion caused by Mercator's projection causes confusion even today.

An Updated World Atlas

A few decades after Mercator's world map came out, a cartographer named Abraham Ortelius published the first new atlas of the world since Ptolemy.

Printed in Antwerp, Belgium, in 1570, the *Theatrum Orbis Terrarum* featured fifty-three maps. It was an instant success. In the new atlas, however, as in other maps of the time, some parts of the world were still fuzzy. For example, mapmakers could not agree on a shape and size for Japan. And without an accurate latitude and longitude grid, the sizes and relationships of the continents to one another were still off. Many countries known today, such as Australia, remained part of terra incognita, the unknown land.

As the map to the left attests, maps of the sixteenth century were often beautifully illustrated. Artists used their imaginations and filled in the gaps in cartographers' knowledge with fanciful beasts.

The new scientific maps were beautifully illustrated, filling in the blank spaces of terra incognita with fanciful images of unusual beasts and plant life. As the unknown areas shrank with each new journey of discovery, mapmakers used the borders of the maps for their decorations instead. These attractive pictures served a social purpose, according to archivist Jeffrey S. Murray. They made new territory inviting. For example, many maps of the New World pictured a countryside and animal life similar to those Europeans would be at home with—rolling hills dotted with forests inhabited by bear and deer, rather than beavers and turkeys. According to Murray, "Such maps would have created a comforting impression of familiarity, rather than strangeness and hostility, for potential investors and settlers." The pretty map illustrations downplayed the presence of Native Americans already living in the lands mapped. Such maps made the New World seem empty and open, fair game ready to be taken over. Their dreams and ambitions fired by the new maps and their illustrations, explorers rose to the occasion and, rightly or wrongly, hurried to stake their claims.

Whatever the justification for their voyages, maps of the Renaissance certainly inspired adventurers and helped them find their way. For navigators, maps did not present a still picture of where they lived, but a changing indicator of where they were headed. During the 1400s, global maps came into sharper focus as a result of the fieldwork of the new breed of explorers. But mapmaking would not be supported financially by entire nations as a legitimate science until the eighteenth century.

Mapping a Nation

Although cartography blossomed during the Age of Exploration, no one had been ambitious enough to organize a detailed survey of an entire nation. Surveying is hard labor, physically and mentally. It involves mapping the shape, size, and position of the landscape by taking calculated measurements. A topographical survey details a region's natural features (such as mountains and lakes) and man-made features (such as bridges and cathedrals). Topographical maps focus on the positions of these features in relation to one another, and how high or low they lie on the land—their elevation.

These exhaustive surveys require enormous amounts of time and money, and they demand sophisticated knowledge of astronomy and mathematics by the surveyor. By the late seventeenth century, however, one nation, France, was thirsty enough to know what lay within its own beloved borders that it spent more than a century on a mission to find the answers. The result was the world's first complete, scientific national survey map. France called it the Carte de Cassini after the family of cartographers who dedicated four generations to its making.

Newton's Theory

In the mid-seventeenth century, the intellectual climate was right for cartography to be considered seriously. However,
great minds were busy debating the globe's shape, not the details of its surface. That the earth was round had been accepted centuries earlier. But with the telescope's invention and growing awareness of the magnetic pull of earth's gravity came a new dilemma: Just how round was round?

By the 1670s, the British scientist Sir Isaac Newton was insisting that the earth was not a perfect sphere. He believed that the earth was slightly flattened at the top and bottom (the poles)

British scientist Isaac Newton insisted that the earth was not a perfect sphere, but slightly flattened at the poles.

and bulged outward a bit at the equator. Newton studied Jupiter and Saturn through his telescope and found that these planets were flattened at the poles and swollen at the equator. Why not earth as well?

Newton's theory interested cartographers because, if it were true, it meant degrees of longitude actually got longer at the poles. It also meant that timekeeping would be a different affair at the equator than at the polar caps, because the earth would spin slightly faster at the equator. Scientifically based maps would have to take the "new" shape of the earth into account if they wanted to preserve accuracy and steer travelers correctly.

Newton was only one of many scientists studying the earth's shape. In France, Louis XIV founded the Académie Royale des Sciences (the Royal Academy of Sciences) in an attempt to woo fine scientific minds the world over. One such thinker was Giovanni Domenico Cassini, an Italian astronomer and cartographer who took on the French name Jean-Dominique. Louis XIV and his chief advisor, Jean-Baptiste Colbert, had grand plans for France. Cassini would help them. The king's ambition was to transform France into Europe's most advanced country, a technological wonder. He envisioned a redesigned nation, built up with roads, bridges, and canals to put the rest of the civilized world to shame. But a designer needs a blueprint. France needed to be mapped accurately before the makeover could start.

The Grand Survey of France Begins with Paris

To kick off the grand survey, the king started with Paris. In the late 1660s, he commissioned astronomer Jean Picard to measure the arc of a meridian (longitude line). The French had chosen this location for their prime, or zero-degree, meridian and based their maps on it.

In the late 1660s, astronomer Jean Picard used telescopic sightings of stars and Jupiter's moons to determine the arc of a meridian (below).

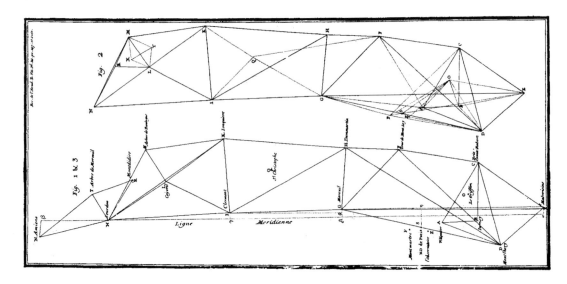

TRIANGULATION

Triangulation was not a new method of measuring the earth's surface. It had been reported as early as 1533. First, the surveyor measured a line between two points on the ground. This was the baseline of an imaginary triangle. Then the surveyor chose a distant but visible landmark to become the third point of the triangle so that the angles of the triangle's other two sides could be calculated. This calculation would show how far away the distant landmark lay from the triangle's base. The method could be repeated to extend a chain of triangles over the land to be surveyed. The difference between early triangulation and that used by Picard was the ability to incorporate precise astronomical sightings, making the triangulation measurements more accurate. And the more precise the measurement, the more detailed and true-to-life the map.

Knowing this meridian's exact arc would help determine a degree of latitude's length by triangulation.

For the surveying of Paris, which took about a decade, Picard and other members of the French Académie used telescope sightings of stars and of Jupiter's moons to determine latitude. They marked the seconds with newly accurate pendulum clocks. The surveyors measured thirteen triangles over seven miles between Paris and Fontainebleau, using wooden rods and special towers erected on hills for triangulation points.

This map of France shows triangulation at the meridian line.

The completed Paris survey map impressed Louis XIV. It set a standard for surveyors to come. According to Simon Berthon and Andrew Robinson:

> It was the first example of a sequence later applied in all great national surveys: first a trigonometrical [based on triangles] skeleton anchored by astronomical observations and baselines, then a topographical survey putting flesh on the skeleton—roads, rivers, bridges, estates and so on.

The French Coastline Survey

Picard followed up his Paris survey with an equally rigorous survey of the French coastline, conducted from 1679 to 1681. The resultant map was a masterpiece, but it uncovered some embarrassing facts. France was actually smaller than its monarch had realized. According to Berthon and Robinson, on seeing the new outline of France, Louis XIV is said to have exclaimed, "Your journey has cost me a major portion of my realm!"

Despite the rude realities they exposed, the scientific surveys caught France's imagination. Picard died, but royal plans were made for Jean-Dominique Cassini to continue surveying where Picard left off until a detailed and accurate map of France had been achieved. Unfortunately, when Colbert, the king's advisor and the driving force behind the surveying project, also died, surveying plans were dropped.

Cassini's World Map

While waiting for the national survey to gear up again, Cassini was hard at work

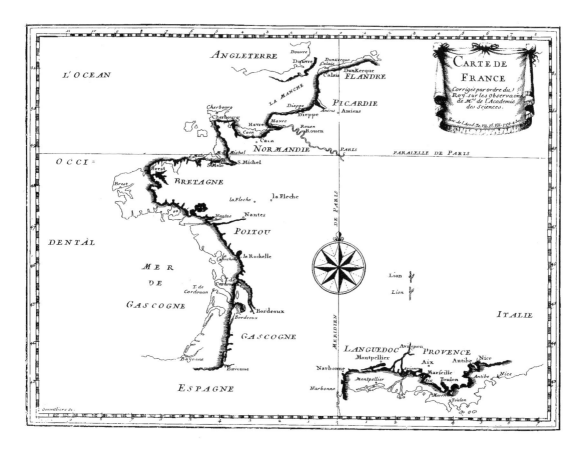

on the most accurate world map yet created. For the first time, hundreds of far-away places were painstakingly drawn based on astronomical observations that allowed the precise fixing of latitude and longitude coordinates. In fact, Cassini allowed no place to be added to his map unless its position had been determined astronomically.

The map in progress was striking. Spreading across the whole floor of a tower in the new Paris Observatory, the twenty-four-foot-wide map looked like a wheel with meridians at 10-degree intervals raying out from its center like spokes. Latitude was drawn in concentric

circles, also 10 degrees apart. The map's circular design caused land masses to distort, but the latitude and longitude of every place was right on target. Cassini had enlisted amateur field-workers the world over to send in data for his calculations. Hundreds of European towns and cities participated and were added to the map. Jesuit missionaries in Egypt, South America, the West Indies, Madagascar, Siam, and China observed eclipses, then reported their findings to Cassini to help pinpoint their exotic locations. Although the Arabs had already correctly determined the length of the Mediterranean Sea, thanks to astronomy, it finally was shown at its correct length on a European map.

Cassini's world map, known as his *planisphére terrestre*, was published in 1696. According to Berthon and Robinson, it became a model for the world maps of the next century. It also helped Cassini get royal approval in 1700 to take up where Picard left off on the national survey. The survey was Cassini's chance to apply scientific methods to the inexact art of mapping, and France's opportunity for glory.

Two Expeditions

Before things got into full swing, however, plans for the survey were delayed while France became embroiled in the continuing controversy over Newton's theory about the earth's shape. According to Berthon and Robinson, in the early 1700s "the figure of the Earth had become . . . the most debated scientific issue of the day, with French and British national pride at stake." In 1735, the French Académie sponsored two separate expeditions to measure the degree of a meridian and determine whether it got shorter or longer nearer the poles. If it were longer, then Newton was right and the earth was flattened at the poles.

One group of scientists headed south to Peru; the other group trekked north to Lapland. Both groups suffered severe hardships. The scientists in Lapland climbed mountaintops in bitter cold and were bitten by huge flies. The scientists who made it to Peru ended up gasping for breath at high altitudes while dodging unfriendly Peruvians who suspected they had really come to ferret out gold. The Lapland expedition completed its triangulation measurements before the other group and returned to France. In 1737, the weary group announced to the Académie that Newton had been right: the poles were flattened.

Ironically, Jean-Dominique Cassini's son Jacques had contended that the opposite was true. He thought the earth might actually be wider at its top and bottom. However, because the earth's shape did not seriously affect maps of smaller areas, the news had little impact on the local mapping he and his son César François (old Cassini's grandson) had conducted while waiting for the expeditions to come home and the national survey to become a priority again. According to Berthon and Robinson, the Cassinis had amazed King Louis XV by completing

a network of four hundred triangles and eighteen baselines, covering France entirely. By 1745 they had a map ready, though without much topographical detail. They followed this with a topographical map of the Low Countries. . . . These maps so impressed Louis XV that he gave the go-ahead to a topographical survey of all

France. The Cassinis began adding rivers, canals, towns, chateaux, vineyards, windmills and watermills, even gallows.

The Carte de Cassini

The Cassini family continued its surveying until 1756, when the king went broke. Determined to keep going, César François Cassini saved the day. He drummed up private investors who would put up funds, then share in the survey's profits. The final maps of the great national survey were finally drawn in 1793. Only César François' son Jean-Dominique, great-grandson of the origi-nal Jean-Dominique, lived to see the unveiling.

The Carte de Cassini represented a unified effort from a country destined to fracture only a year later during the French Revolution's Reign of Terror. The map for this first scientific national survey was laid out on 182 sheets covering an area thirty-six by thirty-six feet. It was the pinnacle of more than one hundred years of scientific—and human—effort. Berthon and Robinson wrote of its reception: "Its military, political and economic value was so obvious that the new government agreed to support publication costs and pay for revisions as they became necessary." The younger

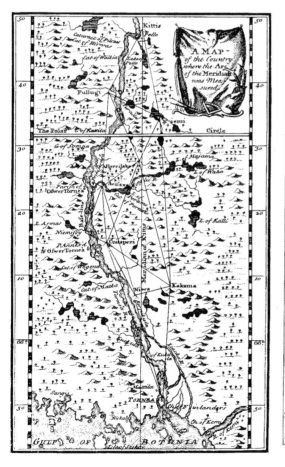

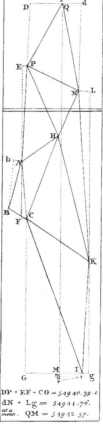

Explorers led an expedition to Lapland in 1735 in an attempt to verify whether the poles were slightly flattened as Newton believed. The map at far left shows the expedition's triangulation measurements. A close-up view appears at right.

Napoléon Bonaparte used Jean-Dominique Cassini's maps and, after the French Revolution, honored the cartographer who had narrowly escaped the guillotine.

Jean-Dominique Cassini, who narrowly escaped the guillotine during the Revolution, was later honored by Napoléon Bonaparte. Napoléon used the Carte de Cassini, among other maps, as a tool of administration and conquest.

Thus the science of cartography became legitimized as, one by one, nations embraced it. According to Lloyd A. Brown, the public began to see mapping as the role of the government rather than of the commercial publisher: "Government surveyors began to assume the role of emissaries in the cause of civic improvement and national solidarity instead of trespassers against the personal rights and civil liberties of the small landholder." Soon after France's national survey, Britain, Austria, and Germany conducted their own surveys. Norway and Sweden followed with their own national surveys in 1815, Russia in 1816, and Denmark and Switzerland in 1830.

As early as 1787, Britain and France joined forces to conduct a joint triangulation measurement across the English Channel. This helped make both countries' maps more exact, and gave a boost to Britain's own national survey, the British Ordnance Survey. But for the most part, nations remained too distrustful of one another to cooperate on international mapping efforts. As

Other nations followed France's lead and performed their own national surveys. The British Ordnance Survey appears below.

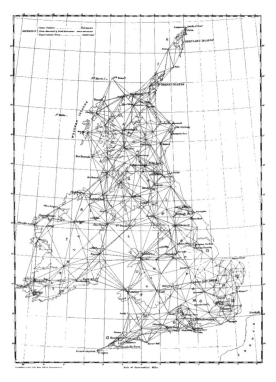

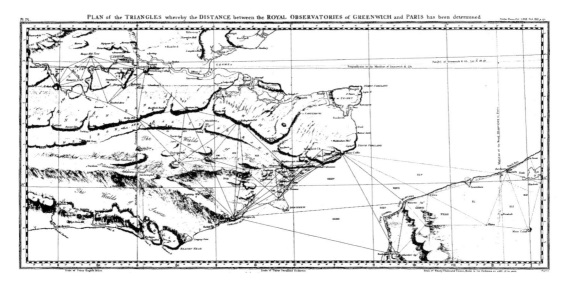

Traditional enemies, France and Britain cooperated in 1787 to survey the English Channel.

Brown comments, "International mapping projects of any size were still suspect and remained so for many years—which was an almost insurmountable barrier to an accurate portrayal of the world as a whole." Even with the infusion of scientific accuracy into the subjectivity of mapmaking, mapping remained shrouded in secrecy. Generally, countries whose policies were the most open to the rest of the world endorsed joint mapping efforts, and those who wished to remain closed off resisted participating. Partly because of this social climate, partly because of technology that was still limited, by the end of the eighteenth century nearly 90 percent of the earth's face remained unmapped. Yet the race was on to fill in the blanks.

Maps Make Rapid Progress

In the nineteenth century, cartography made rapid progress. Worldwide, many governments backed mapping projects, including reconnaissance, or exploratory, mapping of thinly settled continental interiors. Cartographers also experimented with thematic maps. These are maps that communicate facts about their subjects, such as a region's population density or mineral deposits. Mapping such information is called thematic mapping. Both reconnaissance and thematic maps engineered social change.

The most impressive reconnaissance mission in U.S. history was Lewis and Clark's journey west in 1804. In the early 1800s, much of North America did not belong to the United States. Americans competed with Europeans for control of the Pacific Northwest's rich fur trade but knew next to nothing about what lay between the Mississippi River and the Pacific Ocean. A distant war brewing between France and England was soon to launch an ambitious American expedition.

In 1803, the area known as Louisiana was much bigger than the state we know today by that name. It stretched from the Mississippi River all the way to the west coast. At one time,

Cartography made unparalleled advances as the nineteenth century dawned.

the area was under Spanish control. Napoléon Bonaparte forced Spain to return Louisiana to France. However, only a short time later, in April 1803, Napoleon sold the land to the United States because he was afraid the British would capture it. Congress paid France $15,000,000. The purchase added an extra 828,000 square miles to the United States, more than doubling the country's size. Not a bad deal, according to Simon Berthon and Andrew Robinson: "Here was the biggest land sale in history, at a bargain-basement price."

The bargain remained a surprise package to President Thomas Jefferson and the U.S. government. Previous explorers had given them only a vague impression of the territory. A mountain range somehow divided the continent, but the height and extent of these mountains remained shadowy. The Missouri River's westward course was yet uncharted. Jefferson shared the hope of many Americans that the Missouri might somehow cut through the mountains and hook up with the Northwest's Columbia River. If so, people could sail from coast to coast, making access to the Northwest and its valuable fur business that much simpler for American traders. This theoretical river route to the west coast was known as the Northwest Passage.

Lewis and Clark

Anxious to investigate his country's new landholdings, Jefferson hired twenty-nine-year-old Meriwether Lewis and thirty-three-year-old William Clark to lead a detailed surveying expedition. Both men were old hands at wilderness exploring. Lewis was versed in natural

Thomas Jefferson was eager to map the newly purchased Louisiana territory.

history, astronomy, and surveying. A team blessed with both intelligence and diplomacy, Lewis and Clark proved more than equal to the adventure that lay ahead.

President Jefferson had clear expectations for the expedition. He instructed Lewis and Clark to survey the water route up the Missouri and down the Columbia to see if the two rivers mingled. He also wanted them to case out trading possibilities with Native Americans, selling them on the idea that Americans were better business partners than the French, Spanish, or British. And, most importantly for cartography, they were to figure latitude and longitude using astronomy and keep records on birch paper, so that the records would not be damaged by moisture.

In 1804, after estimating the distance to the Pacific coast from longitudes reported in the 1790s, the two captains and their crew headed toward the frontier. Along the route, William Clark showed a talent for making friends with Native Americans. They called him "Red Headed Chief." According to Berthon and Robinson, the cooperation of Native Americans proved crucial to the mission's goal of making accurate maps:

> On the expedition Indians drew maps for [Clark] on a hide or on the ground with charcoal or a piece of stick. This information, which was far more accurate and detailed than from any other source, Clark eventually transferred to a master map of the West. . . . Constantly improved through discussion with Indian delegations and with trappers, this map grew into one of the most important maps ever drawn in America.

Lewis and Clark with Sacajawea, the Native American guide who helped them on their journey. The two men not only possessed intelligence and wilderness experience, they also proved to be adept diplomats, which helped them as they met Native Americans along the way.

Results of the Expedition

In 1806, Lewis and Clark's party returned to announce their findings. The hoped-for water route to the West—the Northwest Passage—was a myth. In fact, the sources of the Columbia and Missouri Rivers were about 220 miles apart. The Rocky Mountains fenced off the West, but the explorers reported that they had discovered five passes through the Rockies into the Pacific Northwest's Oregon Territory. The explorers had also kept careful notes on the climate, plant and animal life, and terrain. These reports and the mapping of them that followed forged a new intimacy between east and west. Americans began to romanticize the West, making the

The Louisiana Purchase offered America a unique opportunity to search for a river route linking east and west. Although Lewis and Clark did not find the fabled Northwest Passage, they accurately mapped the Missouri River, a section of which is shown above.

THE LOUISIANA PURCHASE (1803)

MILES
100 50 0   100   200   300

frontier lands a golden symbol of new hope and new beginnings. The unspoiled West Lewis and Clark described would never be the same.

Americans heading west demanded maps. According to Berthon and Robinson, "[I]n America maps were a crucial aid to white settlement as it spread west, displacing Indians (Native Americans) from the promised land." As cartography became more sophisticated, people became more sophisticated map readers. As Berthon and Robinson point out, only a variety of different maps could suit every would-be traveler's needs:

> [S]ettlers thinking of moving west wanted to know how to get there and what hazards they would face en route. Once there they were interested in the lie of the land if they were planning to farm, the location of minerals if they were prospectors, or the routes of rivers, roads and railroads if they were going into business.

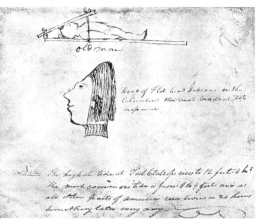

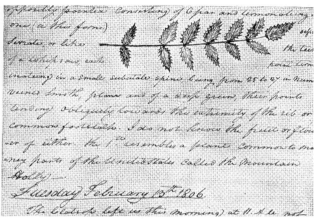

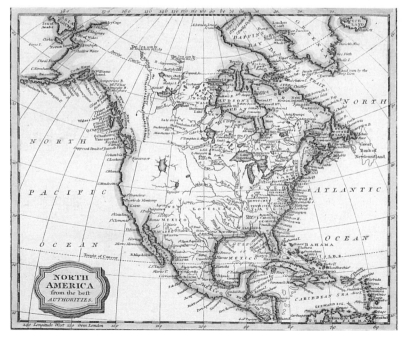

Lewis and Clark took detailed notes on plant life and Native American peoples they met on their important journey (above). Their accurate maps allowed for settlement of the west. (Left) An 1806 map of North America.

As settlers moved west, they needed accurate maps to find their way. (Below) A photograph of Yellowstone canyon. Cartographers were greatly aided by photography, which allowed them to produce maps of areas without actually experiencing them firsthand.

New Technologies Aid Mapping

Cartographers answering the need for detailed maps were helped by two new technologies—the electric telegraph, invented in England in 1838, and photography. During John Wesley Powell's 1869 Colorado River survey, telegraphic time signals from an astronomical station at Salt Lake City, Utah, provided precise data for computing longitude. And photographs provided a rich panorama of images of the West for cartographers and other scientists to draw from. As Berthon and Robinson point out:

> Using photographs, the geologist could study exposed strata in [the] laboratory, the planner in St. Louis or Washington, DC could get an authentic idea of the barren, rocky landscapes facing the new settler; the ethnologist could see what Indians really looked like, shorn of romantic and racist description.

Viewing the West through the unblinking eye of the camera lens helped people see the region realistically. So did the detailed survey mapping of peo-

ple like Powell. The fragility of the desert regions began to be recognized, and national parks such as Yellowstone were established by conservationists against the protests of developers.

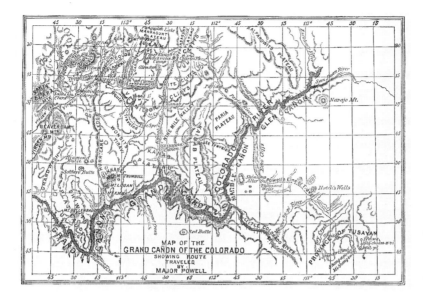

John Wesley Powell surveyed the Colorado River in 1869 to produce this detailed map.

The quality of published maps improved thanks to photography in the second half of the nineteenth century. Norman J.W. Thrower adds that photography also promised a revolution in future mapmaking capabilities: "[P]hotography was soon to provide an improved data source—aerial photography . . . which . . . revolutionized mapping [in the early twentieth century] to as great an extent as did printing in the fifteenth century."

Thematic Mapping

Although the United States was applying intense fieldwork to the creation of detailed topographical maps, Europe was the nineteenth century's leader in thematic mapping. These maps used symbols chosen by the mapmaker to represent ideas like "how much" or "how many." Symbols allowed maps to show the reader factual information such as the amount of rainfall in an area. Cartographers could also manipulate thematic map symbols to show rates of change over time, such as decreases in temperature from summer to winter.

The contour line is one of the earliest examples of a thematic symbol that communicates "how much"—in this case, how much elevation in a region's terrain. Cartographers also used hachures, or shading drawn with tiny lines, to show elevation. But contour lines eventually won out. They could show how quickly an elevation became steep, as well as how high it was. According to Thrower:

> [C]ontours make it possible not only to read elevation, but also to measure slopes within the limit of the contour interval (i.e., vertical distance between successive contour lines). However, the contour method is difficult for some map readers to understand, being a more abstract form of symbolization. The battle for adoption of the contour . . . in topographic mapping was not won as early as 1822.

Showing factual data required a variety of methods from the nineteenth-century mapmaker. The different formats cartographers developed to

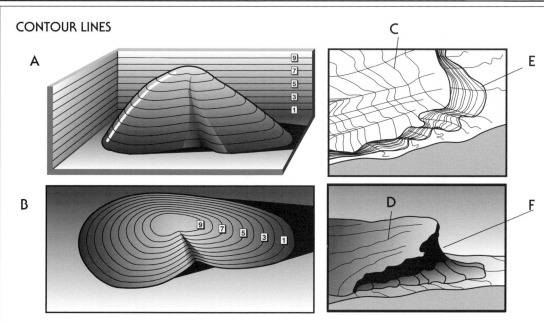

CONTOUR LINES

Contour lines join all points on a map that are at the same height above sea level. To demonstrate contour lines, a model of a mountain can be placed inside a box (A). If water is poured into the box until it is partly full, a line can be drawn around the mountain where the water's edge touches it. More water can then be poured in and the edge of the water line can be traced again. After this process is repeated and the box is emptied of water, the lines remaining are contour lines (B). A map maker decides how far apart, or at what interval, to place contour lines to show the difference in height between each level. Contour lines that are far apart (C) represent fairly flat areas (D), whereas lines that are close together (E) mean hilly or mountainous terrain (F).

meet the challenge are still in use today. Two methods of thematic mapping, the *choropleth* and the dot method, can present very different ideas about a region from the same data, depending on the cartographer's choices before drawing the map.

Choropleth Maps and Dot Maps

Choropleth maps show data divided up according to a region's areas, such as states, counties, or voting precincts. In a dot map, the mapmaker shows "how much" by using dots or other marks, each with assigned values. A single dot can represent one or many units of information, such as one marriage or five hundred tourists. In the nineteenth century, a famous early dot map played a big part in halting an epidemic. In 1854, London was ravaged by an outbreak of cholera. No one was sure how the dreaded disease was transmitted, but Dr. John Snow suspected that it was passed from person to person through their drinking water. Houses had no plumbing. People

CHOROPLETH MAPS

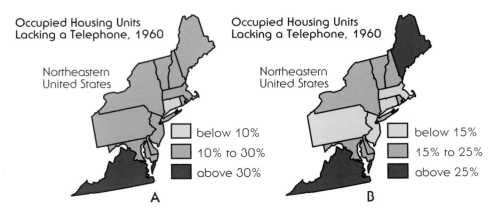

Occupied Housing Units
Lacking a Telephone, 1960

Northeastern
United States

below 10%
10% to 30%
above 30%

A

Occupied Housing Units
Lacking a Telephone, 1960

Northeastern
United States

below 15%
15% to 25%
above 25%

B

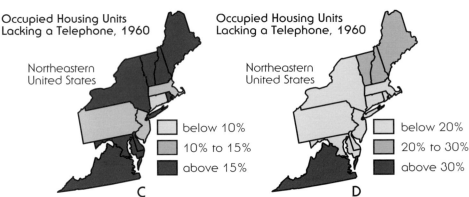

Occupied Housing Units
Lacking a Telephone, 1960

Northeastern
United States

below 10%
10% to 15%
above 15%

C

Occupied Housing Units
Lacking a Telephone, 1960

Northeastern
United States

below 20%
20% to 30%
above 30%

D

Choropleth maps are used to interpret data about related geographic areas at a glance. They do this by translating data into shaded areas that represent high, mid-range, and low amounts. Whether the area is shaded light, dark, or somewhere in between depends on the way the cartographer has chosen to break down the data. It is up to the cartographer to break down the data in a way that conveys a realistic impression about an area. A different set of categories based on the same information can lead to a different map, and possibly a different interpretation of the same facts.

The four choropleth maps shown are all based on the same data: how many northeastern U.S. homes did *not* own a telephone in 1960. The breaks between categories for each map have been changed. In the first map (A), only Virginia appears in the maximum category for homes without phones. However, when the cartographer adjusts the category breaks (B), the number of households with phones seems more evenly distributed. The third map (C) uses categories that suggest that the entire Northeast has limited telephone access, while the last map (D) creates the opposite impression.

Thus, the choropleth map method can easily be manipulated to support different views of the same data, something both map makers and map readers need to bear in mind.

got water by filling buckets at nearby pumps. To test his theory about how cholera was spread, Dr. Snow mapped cholera deaths in the Broad Street area of London for September 1854. He marked the location of each cholera death with a dark block and the location of each water pump with a cross. The map showed the thickest clustering of dark blocks around the area of the Broad Street water pump. When authorities shut the pump down, new cases of cholera in that area decreased dramatically.

Thus, thematic maps proved to be powerful tools that could educate and benefit society. Thrower writes of Snow's famous map: "This map well illustrates the research use of cartography—to find out by mapping that which could not otherwise be learned or, at least, not learned with as great facility and precision."

Mark Monmonier makes an interesting comparison between dot maps and choropleth maps when he asks what would have happened if Snow had used the choropleth instead of the dot method to map his data about cholera deaths. Monmonier shows three different ways of dividing London's Broad Street area into units and assigning intensities to each unit. None of Monmonier's choropleth maps shows the cluster of deaths around the Broad Street pump as clearly as does Snow's dot map. Monmonier comments:

> Areal data [data arranged by area] can yield particularly questionable patterns

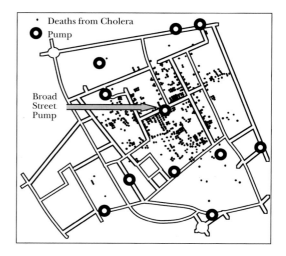

In 1854, Dr. John Snow mapped cholera deaths in an area of London in an attempt to prove that the deaths were linked to contaminated water.

when choropleth maps show rates based on infrequent events, such as deaths from a rare type of cancer. . . . [o]ne question arises whenever the map shows a trend or cluster: Is the pattern real?

The increased variety of nineteenth-century maps created a new awareness of their power. Maps could target the source of an epidemic or inspire settlers to head west. Increasingly, as advancing technology made maps better and easier to use, cartographers had to consider the readers of their maps and how maps could influence people's thoughts and actions. Maps present many points of view, some more accurate and responsible than others. This important fact would become clearer to map readers of the twentieth century as high-tech maps became more complicated.

Twentieth-Century Innovations in Mapping

The end of the nineteenth century marked a turning point for cartography. The spreading net of railways in Europe and the United States had made long-distance travel common. Travelers wanted maps that agreed with each other. Nations realized it would benefit everyone to decide on one prime meridian, the line of longitude on maps assigned the value of zero degrees. If everyone used the same reference point, travel timetables would be consistent and people could do business across wide distances without confusion. In 1884, an international conference met in Washington, D.C. The assembled nations decided that the meridian running through Greenwich, England, would be the prime meridian. They also marked off twenty-four time zones, each 15 degrees of longitude apart. This cooperative effort showed that nations recognized the need to create a world map based on common interests rather than national bias.

The official adoption of the Greenwich meridian signaled society's readiness for a more objective view of the world. In the twentieth century, two major innovations, aerial photography and remote sensing satellites, allowed people to survey the globe from a distance. Seeing earth from a bird's-eye view made it hard to forget that each town, nation, and continent shares its home with every other place. The new mapping revolution shows people that they are all smaller parts of a much larger picture.

The U.S. Geological Survey

The U.S. Geological Survey (USGS), a huge project spanning more than one hundred years, forms a bridge between the two worlds of classic and modern cartography. When it was launched by the U.S. government in 1879, the survey depended on fieldwork. That is, mapping was based on the firsthand observations of people working out in the open, exploring the land up close. By the time the last remote areas of the country were finally mapped in the late 1980s, satellites signaling to computers had rounded up most of the information.

Why did the United States start such a big project? The U.S. Department of the Interior wanted to map the whole country because stampedes of fur trappers, miners, loggers, ranchers, and farmers were racing west into unsettled territory to stake their claims to it, and the government wanted to keep track of what they stumbled on.

The USGS surveyors' task was a painstaking one. Former explorer John Wesley Powell, the survey's first director, divided the countryside into neat chunks, called quadrangles, outlined by parallels and meridians. Each quadrangle had to be mapped to scale, from four miles to the inch for deserts, to one mile to the inch for big cities. The surveyors took notes on the land's geology to include in map overlays.

Today anyone can buy USGS maps at sporting-goods stores and at USGS

WORLD TIME ZONES

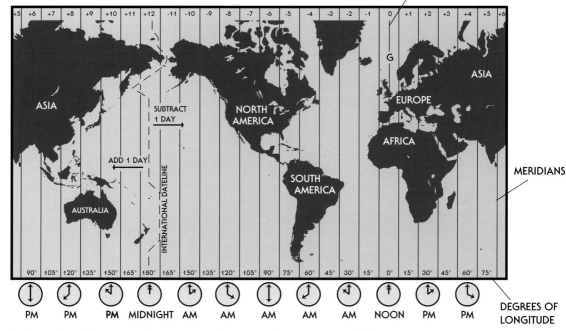

PRIME MERIDIAN OR MERIDIAN OF GREENWICH

MERIDIANS

DEGREES OF LONGITUDE

Before the adoption of international standardized time zones, cities, states, and nations operated with hundreds of different local times. As world transportation and communication systems became more complex, world leaders realized the need for a world map with standardized time zones.

Most people today recognize and use 24 time zones. All places within a given zone use the same time and each zone is one hour ahead of or behind its neighbors. This system enables a person to determine the time almost anywhere on earth.

The time zones are based on the earth's natural rotation. The earth makes one complete rotation every 24 hours. All 360 degrees of the earth's circumference also pass beneath the sun once in 24 hours. Because it takes one hour for the earth to travel 1/24 of 360

degrees, or 15 degrees, a new time zone begins every 15 degrees.

The time zones are marked by imaginary lines of longitude called meridians. Meridians run north and south along the surface of the earth, from the North Pole to the South Pole. The meridian that runs through Greenwich, England, serves as a common starting point for determining time and east and west directions. The Meridian of Greenwich, also known as the Prime Meridian, is located at zero degrees longitude. Halfway around the world, at 180 degrees longitude, is the International Date Line. These two lines mark the world's two halves or hemispheres and they are exactly 12 time zones apart. This means that when it is noon at Greenwich, it is midnight at the International Date Line.

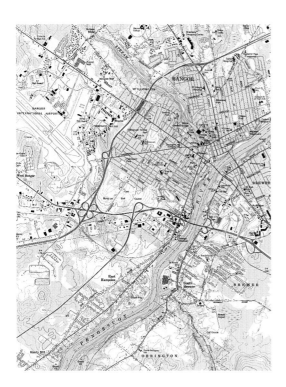

A portion of a U.S. Geological Survey (USGS) map of Maine reveals the immense amount of detailed information a modern map contains.

field offices. Modern wilderness explorers prefer the map series drawn to seven-and-a-half-minute scale. These maps show quadrangles covering seven and one-half minutes of a degree of longitude and latitude. (There are sixty minutes in a degree.) According to writer John Barsness, "The scale works out to about 2.5 inches per mile, enough detail to show city streets and small ponds." If you spread out this map series end to end, it would form a map of the United States the size of four football fields. The effort of compiling the USGS survey was staggering. That it was even attempted, let alone finished, shows one country's commitment to making the discoveries of cartography available to everyone. Without old-fashioned fieldwork joining forces

with high technology, the survey might have remained John Wesley Powell's dream. Instead, in the twentieth century, it became a reality.

Aerial Photography

In the 1930s, aerial photography, a technique of taking photos of the ground from airplanes that had been developed during World War I, was perfected. Aerial photography was a major landmark in cartography's history because it meant that information for maps did not have to be gathered on the ground. Areas that were difficult for field-workers to reach could be observed from the air.

Aerial photographs are taken from airplanes flying across an area of land in a series of straight lines. A large number of photos are taken at short distances apart. According to Jean-Philippe Grelot, "Each section of terrain flown over is photographed twice, from different angles. In this way the aerial photographs provide the binocular effect of human vision, which makes possible the appreciation of distance and relief." The resulting photographs have a three-dimensional effect, as though the viewer were looking down from on high, similar to Ptolemy's vision of the godlike viewpoint.

How is a map made from an aerial photograph? Cartographers use a science called photogrammetry, a branch of engineering that applies photographic measurement to mapping. An engineer looks at two aerial photographs of the same area, taken in order, through an optical machine. The machine has two eyepieces, one focused on each photograph. The engineer traces the land's contours on a drafting table to record them. Before printing, the resulting map is checked for accuracy by actual fieldwork. As Sebastian Junger explains, "Features that are hard to distinguish on a photo must be identified in person. Even a spy photo would not show a dirt road beneath dense tree cover. Field workers must go out and check these details." It takes roughly two years to transform an aerial photograph into a printed map.

Aerial photographs have not replaced maps. As Thrower points out, the photographic process can distort and misrepresent scale. But more importantly, photos simply show too much information. Part of the art of mapmaking is deciding which features to include and which to leave out, depending on what the map will be used for. But even though aerial photography has not replaced mapping, it has

become a powerful map-making tool, according to Thrower: "Photogrammetric methods have reduced the cost of making maps remarkably, make it possible to map areas that would otherwise be difficult to reach and, most important, increased the quality and accuracy of mapping generally."

Remote Sensing Satellites

Space-age technology has brought a new precision to cartography. To observe the world more carefully, humans have launched small spacecraft called remote sensing satellites into orbit around the planet. These quiet watchers train powerful scanners, devices similar to the human eye, on the earth's surface. The scanners pick up the changing patterns of electromagnetic radiation the earth gives off. The kind

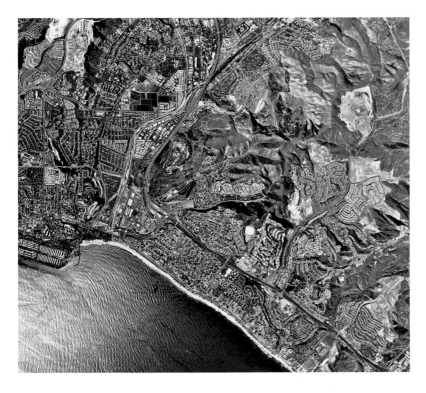

Aerial photography freed cartographers from having to survey land on the ground to make detailed maps. At left is an aerial photograph of a portion of southern California.

of radiation depends on the environ-ment: temperature, humidity, vegeta-tion, rock formations. The satellite then transmits the earth conditions it "saw" to waiting computers at a ground station, in either photographic or nu-merical form, where the data are inter-preted by humans. Today, through remote sensing technology, people can see the earth from a totally new per-spective.

The United States and France are leaders in satellite capability. NASA launched Landsat 1 in 1972. Currently, Landsats 4 and 5 can pinpoint objects the size of a baseball diamond from seven hundred miles above the planet, according to writer Gregory T. Pope. SPOT 2, managed by the French space agency, can make out landmarks as small in area as thirty-two feet.

Other types of aerial photography aid cartographers. One of the most remarkable innovations in the quest for accurate maps is the satellite. The image of San Francisco, California (above), was taken by Landsat, while the closeup of Dallas, Texas (right), was taken by SPOT.

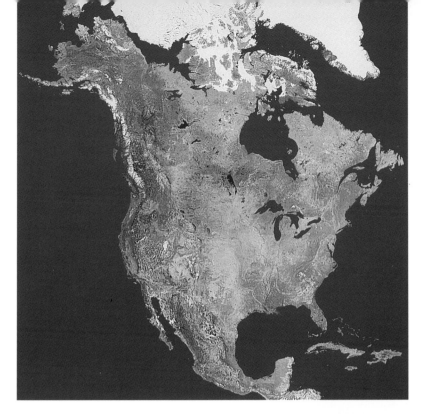

Satellite photography is remarkable in its ability to pick up the tiniest images as well as entire continents. (Left) An image of North America taken by Landsat. (Below) An artist's depiction of a remote sensing satellite used by cartographers.

Uses of Remote Sensing Data

Remote sensing has streamlined map updating to a matter of months rather than years. The earth's surface is always changing, and satellites can quickly record these changes. This has made maps based on satellite data more efficient tools. For example, the French have sold SPOT-scanned quadrangles of the United States to update USGS survey maps that have fallen far out-of-date.

In addition to providing information for land management and development, remote sensing data can collect global environmental data. According to Gregory T. Pope, maps based on satellite images can show developers and environmentalists the changing locations of endangered wilderness areas:

> Trees and tar, cornfields and concrete reflect the sun's radiation in distinctive spectral signatures that SPOT can mea-

sure. The U.S. Fish and Wildlife Service used a SPOT image to draw a vegetation base map of the Great Dismal Swamp National Wildlife Refuge, which straddles the Virginia-North Carolina border, in order to trace the shifting industrial and agricultural areas around the refuge. Meanwhile, planning new roads around Jacksonville, the Florida Department of Transportation employed SPOT data to distinguish sensitive wetlands from resilient uplands.

As with aerial photography, remote sensing satellites have not replaced real people when it comes to mapping detail. Satellites can spot streets and rivers, but ground-based surveying teams must still investigate and record features like fences or manholes. The human input of fieldwork is still very much a part of modern mapping, as Pope comments: "Ground-based surveying teams . . . have traditionally fixed small features onto maps and continue to do so. Until remote-sensing satellites become more eagle-eyed, their jobs are safe."

The Global Positioning System

People have been asking "Where in the world am I?" since the dawn of time. But until the recent development of the Global Positioning System (GPS), they had to make do with compasses. Now a new type of handheld device can act as a turbocharged compass when it picks up the pulses broadcast from four of twenty-four GPS satellites circling the planet. Working with data beamed down by the satellites, the palm-sized receiver can calculate a traveler's longitude and latitude, the speed he or she is moving, the direction to head to reach

a destination, and how long it will take to get there. GPS receiving units can store locations, allowing a traveler to plot a course from one location to another. The receivers have been available to consumers since the early 1990s; by 1993 they sold for about $600. As technology improves, the price is likely to go down and eventually will probably be as common as the handheld calculator.

Each GPS satellite is about the size of a car and orbits the earth every twelve hours at an altitude of over ten thousand miles, continuously transmitting radio signals showing its position and the time according to an onboard atomic clock. The satellites were developed by the U.S. Defense Department, beginning in the late 1970s, at a cost of more than $3 billion. The military wanted to be able to position soldiers

A hiker checks her position using a handheld receiver that actually transmits information directly from Global Positioning System (GPS) satellites.

GPS receivers intercept two different signals, one for civilians and one for the military. A driver checks her location using a GPS receiver (left). Soldiers used GPS technology during the Persian Gulf War to keep track of troop positions in the vast Iraqi desert.

and guide computer-driven weapons to their targets. During the Persian Gulf War, allied troops equipped with GPS receivers could keep track of each other in the vast Iraqi desert.

Two Types of Signals

However, because foreign powers and civilians can also pull in GPS signals, the satellites send out two different sets of pulses, one for the military and one for civilians. Military signals allow receivers to fix their positions to within about fifty feet, while the civilian signal locates its receivers to within one hundred feet. According to science writer Robert Naeye, during wartime, the air force can weaken the civilian signal even further so that enemy armies could only fix positions to within a mile.

The Global Positioning System is not just for military maneuvering. GPS technology helps hikers find their way back to base camp. Delivery services hook up with GPS signals to send their trucks along the fastest routes. Commercial airlines use GPS satellite data to help guide their jumbo jets, reducing the chance of crashes. Already, GPS receivers have been hooked up to laptop computers, allowing travelers to watch their progress on a scrolling on-screen map. GPS technology has captured the public imagination.

The Geographic Information System

Remote sensing technology's major contribution to cartography has been the development of a completely new type of map: the Geographic Information System (GIS). When satellites feed their data to computers, special software translates spatial features (houses, street intersections, rivers) into points, lines, and geometric shapes. These symbols are stored in a computer's database. According to Pope, "Using a GIS, cartographers can analyze geographic information without ever looking at a

GLOBAL POSITIONING SYSTEM

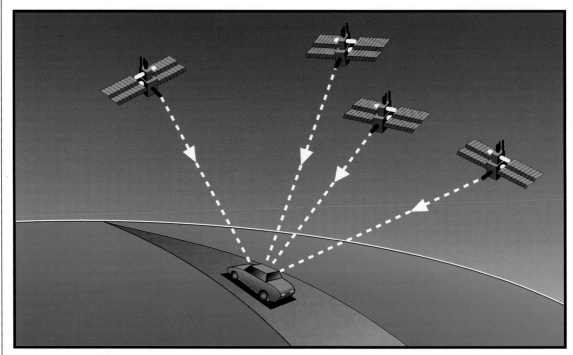

The Global Positioning System, developed by the U.S. Department of Defense, is a network of satellites and receivers working together to help people pinpoint their locations or track moving objects anywhere on the globe.

The system uses highly accurate clocks and computers aboard orbiting satellites and in GPS receivers on earth. A GPS satellite's onboard computer constantly generates a string of numbers that broadcast its identity and position. The satellite is also equipped with an onboard atomic clock that keeps the coded transmission on a strict schedule.

When satellites beam the coded signals to earth, a GPS receiver with its own clock and computer generates a matching code. By measuring the time lag between its own code and the arrival of an identical satellite code, the receiver calculates its distance from the satellite. Similar information from four different

satellites allows the receiver to pinpoint its own position anywhere on the globe. The results are amazingly precise. Military troops consulting handheld GPS receivers have been able to pinpoint their locations to within sixteen meters, for example.

GPS technology is a valuable defense tool, but it also has great commercial potential. Hikers can consult GPS receivers to keep from getting lost. Delivery trucks and ambulances can use GPS to report their positions to dispatchers, who can then route them more efficiently. Airlines can use GPS to allow jumbo jets to take off and land more safely and efficiently. Intelligent vehicle-tracking systems installed under car hoods might someday show drivers their locations on dashboard computer screens. GPS may even be instrumental in predicting earthquakes, say geologists who use the technology to measure subtle changes in the earth's surface.

map. Or they can unleash snazzy graphics routines to display the information in a more familiar maplike form."

Using computers to make maps has revolutionized the commercial mapmaking business. According to Pope:

> The . . . mapmaking houses, whose profits hinge on the exactitude of their products, have wholeheartedly embraced GIS technology largely because keying corrected digital data into a computer takes a lot less time than the traditional chore of scribing a whole new map onto a sheet of coated film.

Far more than just an easier way to draw a map, GIS technology has opened up new ways of seeing in many fields. Computerized maps are used in scientific research, business marketing, and urban planning. In Huntsville, Alabama, the community wanted to combine its many separate and confusing maps for tax assessment, property lines, police precincts, water and sewer lines, and so on, into one computerized package. Using remote sensing technology, they came up with a photographic map detailed enough to show tiny landmarks. The photographic map was loaded into a computer. Custom maps of different topics could then be called up by city planners as needed. Huntsville has used GIS to identify parts of town that are too steep or too fragile for proposed construction projects.

The U.S. Geological Survey operates a GIS research laboratory. According to Pope, in 1987, the U.S. Forest Service called on the GIS laboratory for help when a mining company approached them about starting an open-pit copper mine in Arizona's Prescott National Forest. Researchers at the GIS laboratory loaded a computer with elevation data; a Landsat satellite image; and data from paper maps showing geology, land ownership boundaries, and the proposed mine plan. The computer generated a three-dimensional view showing the mine pits and how they would affect drainage and stand out as an eyesore along a nearby scenic drive. The GIS analysis convinced the Forest Service to turn down the mining company deal.

Computers have revolutionized this USGS worker's job. Special software can now translate satellite information, allowing cartographers to analyze the information without ever looking at a map.

Modern Maps Express Human Viewpoints

Even though computerized maps based on satellite data are far more accurate than old-fashioned maps, they are still reflections of the ideas of the people who make them. Geographer Denis Wood explains that often cartographers change the appearance of satellite photos to turn them into pictures of the earth that, like maps, can be read clearly. Sometimes the cartographer pieces together different pixels, or parts of a computerized photograph, from different satellite images taken at different times, creating a sort of mosaic that adds up to a unified picture.

Wood points to the "GeoSphere" map designed by Tom Van Sant and Lloyd Van Warren, a global map that was crafted by picking and choosing images from satellite photographs. In many cases, writes Wood, Van Sant erased, adjusted, or switched the satellite data for the purpose of making a clear, easy-to-read map of the earth. This map does not duplicate a view of the planet from space. For example, a major feature of the earth seen from space is a covering of clouds. To make the entire earth's surface visible, Van Sant rejected images where clouds blocked the view of the land. If cloud-free images were not available, Van Sant artificially subtracted the clouds, leaving, as Wood writes, "an exposed earth whose continental outlines have been defined by an impartial, electronic eye."

By artificially combining many different satellite images, cartographers can choose the features of the land that they would like to emphasize. In the GeoSphere map, Van Sant found separate images of winter snowcaps and of summer vegetation and placed them together on the same view of the globe. A single satellite photo of the earth's surface would not be able to show how the

Tom Van Sant and Lloyd Van Warren combined many different satellite photographs to produce this GeoSphere map. The cartographers manipulated the satellite images to produce one clear, easy-to-read picture that combined winter snowcaps and summer vegetation.

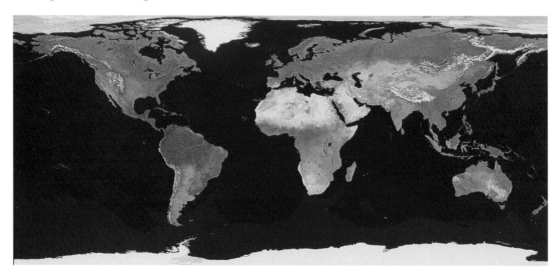

earth looks in both summer and winter at the same time. But with the help of Van Sant's piecing together of different views, an image was created that showed the most brightly colored vegetation and heaviest snowfall. This made a vivid, clear picture that helped viewers see the earth's major surface features clearly. Wood explains:

> For low and moderate latitudes, the map's creators selected images showing the most pronounced summer vegetation, for high latitudes and altitudes, they chose images that highlighted winter snowfall. River systems have been thickened to make them visible, and false color was applied. . . . All these decisions serve a useful purpose in that they emphasize certain aspects of the earth, thereby making the Van Sant map more useful and easier to read than it would be otherwise. But one should keep in mind that the absence of clouds, the extent of the vegetative cover, the visibility of the rivers and all the colors seen on the map are expressions of the mapmakers' vision, not attributes intrinsic to the earth itself.

Thus, with the help of new technology, mapmakers can rearrange and manipulate computer images, putting them together in new ways to communicate messages to the viewer interested in learning about the planet. Map readers need to remember that a satellite photo is often constructed of many images chosen by the cartographer. It is not an actual snapshot of the globe. Viewers of satellite-photo maps also need to bear in mind that, just because these global presentations were created with sophisticated scientific techniques, they do not necessarily present a complete, exact picture. As with aerial photography, things can be left out or distorted, whether accidentally or delib-

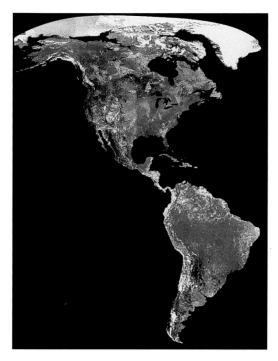

If used by a cartographer, this satellite image of North and South America would likely be manipulated via computer to enhance certain features.

erately to emphasize the map's purpose. People tend to assume that the more high-tech a map is, the more exact it is. No map can be completely accurate. Each map is an interpretation of the mapmaker's idea of the truth. Maps cannot show everything; if they could, they would be too confusing to be useful. According to Wood, "Viewers should be better educated about what maps can and cannot do."

The spirit of global cooperation that began the twentieth century with the Greenwich meridian decision has led to a global network of satellites and computers working together to present a clearer picture of the world. The new cartography has been called a crystal ball because of the vision it holds for the future.

Mapping the Future

Now that cartography has been revolutionized by high technology, humans need no longer limit their view of the world to what they can see in front of them. Maps have the potential to broaden a person's perspectives. They also have the power to distort a person's view of the world. Whether maps help or harm future generations all depends on how we look at them.

According to Simon Berthon and Andrew Robinson, remote sensing satellites and the computers that process the huge amounts of information that satellites collect have made cartography not national, not continental, but truly global in scope. Berthon and Robinson point out that the whole world has the ability to work together on global projects like exploring the Pacific Ocean floor, investigating the holes in the ozone layer over Antarctica, predicting earthquakes in California, monitoring U.S. airline flight patterns, documenting the incidence of AIDS in New York City, or determining the impact of global warming on the European coastline. These are projects that can affect

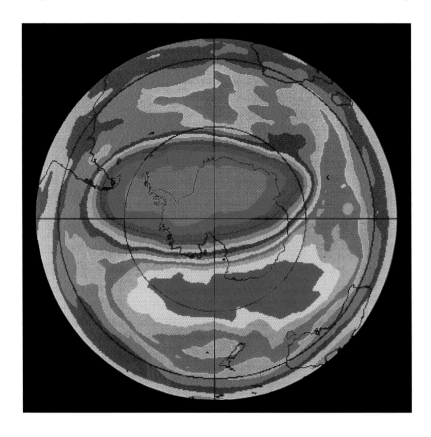

Mapmaking has become a truly global effort. Using images such as this one of the ozone hole over Antarctica, scientists can work together in international efforts.

In the future, GPS may be used to make everyday activities such as crop spraying more efficient and safe.

the entire planet, and the new cartography can help humans sort out observations, find patterns within the problems, and also may point in the direction of solutions.

Gregory T. Pope comments on the importance of maps to the future:

> More precise than ever before, thanks to computerization and satellite imagery, modern maps no longer stop at simply guiding the user from point to point. Like crystal balls, they must let the user gaze into the future to answer thorny questions: where to site a landfill, how to route a fleet of ambulances, how the terrain will look after an earthquake has rippled through.

The Future of the Global Positioning System

The Global Positioning System satellites, with their ability to guide anyone or anything in motion, are the navigators of the future. GPS technology can create safer, more efficient airplane flight paths, for instance. The Federal Aviation Administration is investigating the use of GPS signals that would inform every pilot, air-traffic controller, and FAA center of the location of every airplane in flight. This way, planes could safely fly closer together when

making landings. Someday, GPS could even direct planes making automatic landings in dense fog.

Agriculture has found a potential use for GPS that could help the environment as well, according to business writer Paul M. Eng. Aerial crop sprayers could avoid overspraying and overfertilizing by keeping track of where they have already flown over a crop field by using GPS. The satellite readings could make the spreading of fertilizers and pesticides much more efficient than they are now, saving money and reducing pollution.

As a navigational aid, GPS is a natural for the automobile industry. Chrysler and General Motors are just two companies looking into installing GPS receivers and tracking screens as options on their cars of the future. The way it works is simple: GPS technology is combined with computerized land maps, such as road maps, to set up an intelligent vehicle tracking system. Drivers could glance at a small dashboard computer screen to find the best route. The screen could alert drivers to upcoming traffic jams and display ways to avoid them. It could even be programmed to show the location of the nearest automated bank teller machine for the driver a little low on cash. But installing GPS in cars is not just an amusing luxury option; it could save lives. GPS receivers could be installed under car hoods and equipped with radio transmitters. In case of a car accident, the transmitter could automatically broadcast the car's position to the police. This could be especially crucial to drivers frequenting deserted country roads.

The last scenario is an example of linking the locating capability of GPS with communications technology. This link is the wave of the future, according to writer and Manhattan Institute senior fellow Peter Huber:

> Communicating GPS can be the ultimate flashing light for people (like truck

drivers or jet pilots) who need to report their position to others. Hijacking the 18-wheeler or snatching a Corvette is going to get a lot riskier when tiny positioning transmitters can be concealed anywhere in the vehicle. If you want to track migratory birds, prisoners on parole, or (what amounts to much the same thing) a teenage daughter in possession of your car keys, you are going to be a customer sooner or later.

The Future of Computerized Maps

The Geographic Information System, the databases that store the information

The Geographic Information System, the databases that store the information beamed down from satellites, makes it possible to keep constant track of the changing environment. These computer-generated images show the effect of global warming.

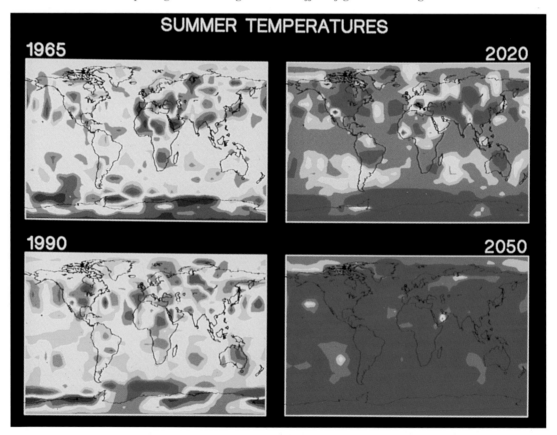

beamed down from remote sensing satellites, makes it possible to keep constant track of the changing nature of the planet. GIS maps can select from a huge amount of information to show people a picture of a particular piece of the world puzzle. Because GIS can process data so rapidly, it is ideal for scientific use. In the future, scientists hope to use GIS to merge data from various satellites to keep track of major trends such as global climate changes.

Even though GIS can store more data than can be displayed understandably on a single paper map, it will not replace paper maps. In fact, it will probably spawn a new breed of paper map: With GIS, people can create made-to-order, one-time maps, custom-designed for specific tasks. This capability appeals to U.S. Geological Survey officials, according to writer Sebastian Junger:

> The official dream of the main USGS office . . . is that geographical data for the entire country will eventually be stored digitally. Buying a map will entail specifying not just the quadrangle but also what you want on it: latitude and longitude, contour lines, mineral rights. The computer will then print your tailor-made map while you wait.

The new availability of technical information on easy-to-follow maps will give the average citizen as well as the land-use planner or the developer the tools to make informed decisions. Before people start a major construction project, for example, they can ask themselves, "How will this affect the land?" Custom maps can provide the answers.

As GIS technology becomes cheaper, more people will have computerized databases for creating maps at their fingertips. According to writer Gregory T. Pope, mapmakers and users

will need to be aware of where their data came from. GIS technology makes it easy to combine data, which can affect the accuracy of a map. Out-of-date information, or information that was compiled for a different purpose, can be used through GIS to create an official-looking map that may mislead its readers. This brings up the question of who is responsible when a map steers readers in the wrong direction. Pope quotes the example of a map put together from census data that is used to route emergency vehicles. If the ambulance gets lost on a dead-end street that did not appear on the map, whose fault is it? Presumably, the mapmaker would be liable, not the census department or the ambulance driver. This type of situation is much more likely in the era of GIS, because making the mistake of feeding old or mismatched data into GIS is so simple to do. Cartographers must consider potentially dangerous situations when they choose the sources with which they design their maps.

An Important Tool

Cartographers do not create or solve social problems, nor do the maps they make. But mapmakers are responsible for the quality of their maps. The new GIS technology makes it easier for anyone to become an amateur cartographer. For example, census data that charts block-by-block analyses of population, voting-age population, and racial makeup once had to be looked up in volumes available from public library reference desks or government printing offices. American citizens fortunate enough to have a computer loaded with a GIS database can study

International events have a great impact on maps. The reunification of Germany suddenly made every map of Europe that showed a divided Germany obsolete.

this information at their leisure. Working from their personal viewpoints about the statistics, they can then create a variety of maps with a flick of a switch or two. Mapmakers and map readers alike should be careful to understand the data processed by GIS technology and remember that maps can mislead readers if they are not responsibly constructed.

According to Pope, any citizen can consult GIS databases, such as those containing census information, for example. By using GIS data, citizens can become more active in their government's decision-making process. When people buy GIS databases or consult them for free in public libraries, they can easily uncover the same facts politicians have access to. Using the tool of GIS technology can inspire people to work harder to come up with solutions to national, even global, problems. GIS databases make it easier for people to see patterns and respond to them, he suggests.

Keeping Track of Changing Boundaries

The new digital mapping can be used not only for monitoring local population shifts, but for keeping track of national upheavals as well. Recent events have shown that the political boundaries of nations can change rapidly. Future maps will be able to use computer technology to respond to these changes much more efficiently. When the National Geographic Society was getting the presses ready to publish the sixth edition of its world atlas, only months before the reunification of East and West Germany, it had to decide whether to show one or two countries. The society consulted with the German governments and decided to print the atlas showing a united Germany with two capital cities. The National Geographic Society had already printed 240,000 copies before receiving word from Germany that it wanted its capital shown as Berlin only. The thousands of maps featuring the dual capital were rendered useless, and new maps showing one Germany with the capital city of Berlin had to be made quickly. Because GIS can process information quickly and eliminates the need for time-consuming redrawing of maps, last-minute revisions might be more easily made in the future using GIS technology.

Awareness of the Subjectivity of Maps

As mapping technology advances, people will become more sophisticated map users. They will be more likely than ever to realize that all maps are subjective. This means that they are affected by the personal views, experiences, and backgrounds of their makers. Today, most people are not as conscious as they someday may be of how their own thinking can affect their perception of the world and the way people draw maps.

For example, in an early 1990s study conducted by geographer Thomas F. Saarinen and reported by science writer Richard Monastersky, first-year college students in twenty cities around the world were asked to draw a world map. The results did not look much like reality. No matter where they lived, students from every continent enlarged the size of Europe and shrank Africa. Most people placed Europe in the center, suggesting that they thought Europe was the most important continent. Monastersky believes some of the responsibility for these distortions lies with the most popular world map, the Mercator

projection. The Mercator's tendency to enlarge the size of some landmasses, like Europe and Greenland, and shrink the size of others, like Africa and South America, may be partly responsible for the college students' misconceptions about the world map. But he also believes people carry mental maps in their heads that reflect their ignorance about other lands. This ignorance could interfere with friendly relationships between countries.

The Mercator Projection Sparks Controversy

The Mercator projection map is more than four hundred years old, and it is the image of the world most familiar to American students. Because it distorts landmasses, the map may influence the way students perceive other cultures, according to Salvatore Natoli of the National Council for Social Studies. Natoli argues, "In our society we unconsciously equate size with importance and even with power, and if the Third World countries are misrepresented, they are likely to be valued less."

According to writer Scott Minerbrook, the unavoidable distortions in all flat maps of the globe have recently become a target of political attention. American educators and publishers, as well as the World Council of Churches and several United Nations organizations, are promoting a map to replace the old Mercator, called the Peters projection. The map was created in the 1970s by German historian and cartographer Arno Peters. According to Minerbrook, Peters claims to present landmasses more accurately. Peters has criticized the cartographic profession's use of the Mercator map, implying that mapmakers have intentionally used the Mercator projection's distortions to foster European world dominance.

The Peters map also has flaws, however. According to Minerbrook, "All maps distort reality. Flattening a spherical world without misrepresenting some part of it is simply not possible." Peters tries to represent the sizes of land masses in relation to one another more fairly, but in the process, some countries are still stretched out of shape. On Peters's map, Africa and South America look longer, rather than smaller, than they really are.

Because of the technical flaws in Peters's map, and because of his radical views, most cartographers disapprove of the Peters projection. However, others are convinced of its educational value.

According to Minerbrook, in October 1990 HarperCollins Publishers released the first American edition of a world atlas based on the Peters projection. And many schools are now using the Peters map to teach students about map distortions and about the strong European emphasis on the Mercator map. In fact, the Texas Education Agency has declared that textbook publishers who sell books to Texas students must explain that the world does not really resemble the world presented by the Mercator projection map. New textbooks purchased for Texas students must contain examples of a variety of different map projections to make this point. The controversy over the Mercator projection has sparked a healthy discussion of the way map projections can influence people's opinions about the world. The de-

Many people believe this world map by Arno Peters depicts the size of the continents more accurately and fairly than the Mercator map. According to writer Scott Minerbrook, however, "All maps distort reality."

With all of the amazing technology that allows maps to present ever more detailed and varied information, maps still help people answer the age-old question, "Where am I?"

bate over how maps represent the nations and populations of the globe is likely to continue well into the future.

Maps once charted the course of ships. In the future, they will indicate the changing course of the planet's destiny. In humanity's search to find its way in the universe, people will turn to maps. With maps, we draw pictures of future plans, future worlds. Our maps will document the course we have set for ourselves.

Glossary

■■

aerial photography: A technique of taking overlapping photographs of the ground from airplanes for mapping purposes.

astrolabe: An instrument for measuring distance and location whose rotating arm is lined up with a star to determine the angle of elevation.

cartography: The science of mapmaking.

choropleth map: A map in which color or shading is applied to areas bounded by statistical or administrative limits.

compass: A device for determining direction by use of a pivoting magnetic needle.

contour: An imaginary line connecting all points on a map that are the same elevation.

contour interval: The vertical distance between two contour lines next to each other.

dead reckoning: A nonscientific way of navigating based on experience and intuition.

distortion: Change in shape of object being mapped, caused by transforming part of a round surface onto a flat surface.

dot map: A map of earth phenomena in which each dot represents a specific number of the distribution being mapped.

gnomon: A straight rod whose cast shadow is used to calculate latitude.

Greenwich meridian: The line of longitude chosen in 1884 as the prime meridian, assigned the value of zero degrees on maps.

grid: A reference system on a map of two sets of parallel lines intersecting at right angles, forming squares.

hachure: A short line running in the direction of a slope to show a landscape's relief.

omphalos syndrome: Believing one's society is at the center of the universe.

orthogonal: Evenly patterned, such as a grid pattern.

photogrammetry: A branch of engineering that applies the measuring of photographs to mapping.

portolan chart: Precise maps showing the features of the Mediterranean coastline, used by navigators beginning in the thirteenth century.

projection: Any systematic arrangement of meridians and parallels of the curving surface of a spheroid on a flat surface.

reconnaissance mapping: The mapping of sparsely settled continental interiors during the nineteenth century.

surveying: Mapping the shape, size, and position of the landscape by taking calculated measurements.

T-O map: The most popular Christian world map of the Middle Ages, showing Jerusalem in the center, an O-shaped ocean, and a T shape of rivers separating three continents.

terra incognita: Latin for "unknown land."

thematic map: A map that locates the distribution of a single feature, such as population, of an area.

topographic map: A map of the land's surface, showing physical features (such as hills) and cultural features (such as roads and administrative boundaries).

triangulation: A method of finding a position or location on earth. It is done by dividing a part of the earth's surface into triangles, then using the triangles and measurements from two fixed points a known distance apart to find a point on earth.

For Further Reading

William F. Allman, "A Sense of Where You Are," *U.S. News & World Report*, April 15, 1991.

Simon Berthon and Andrew Robinson, *The Shape of the World: The Mapping and Discovery of the Earth*. Chicago: Rand McNally, 1991.

Paul M. Eng, "Who Knows Where You Are? The Satellite Knows," *Business Week*, February 10, 1992.

Peter Huber, "An Ultimate Zip Code," *Forbes*, August 31, 1992.

Mark Lewyn, "Where Am I? Ask a Satellite," *Business Week*, October 26, 1992.

Scott Minerbrook, "The Politics of Cartography," *U.S. News & World Report*, April 15, 1991.

Richard Monastersky, "The Warped World of Mental Maps," *Science News*, October 3, 1992.

Robert Naeye, "The Right Time and Place," *Discover*, January 1994.

Gregory T. Pope, "The New Cartographers," *Omni*, December 1991.

Peter Ryan, *Explorers and Mapmakers*. New York: E.P. Dutton, 1990.

Scholastic Magazine, "Charting the Course," September 20, 1991.

U.S. News & World Report, "Q & A" [Interview with cartographer John Garver], November 26, 1990.

Additional Works Consulted

Leo Bagrow, *History of Cartography.* Revised and enlarged by R.A. Skelton. Cambridge, MA: Harvard University Press, 1964.

John Barsness, "Topo Maps: Where We're Headed," *Field and Stream,* June 1993.

Lloyd A. Brown, *The Story of Maps.* Boston: Little, Brown, 1949.

G. R. Crone, *Maps and Their Makers.* London: Hutchinson and Co., 1952, 1962.

Catherine Delano-Smith, "Imagining the World," *Unesco Courier,* June 1991.

Samuel Y. Edgerton Jr., "From Mental Matrix to Mappamundi to Christian Empire: The Heritage of Ptolemaic Cartography in the Renaissance," in David Woodward, ed., *Art and Cartography: Six Historical Essays.* Chicago: University of Chicago Press, 1987.

Jean-Philippe Grelot, "The Perspective from Space," *Unesco Courier,* June 1991.

J. B. Harley, "The New History of Cartography," *Unesco Courier,* June 1991.

Sebastian Junger, "The Last Map Makers," *American Heritage,* September 1991.

Mark Monmonier, *How to Lie with Maps.* Chicago: University of Chicago Press, 1991.

Jeffrey S. Murray, "Fanciful Worlds," *Canadian Geographic,* September/October 1993.

———, "Maps That Deceive," *Canadian Geographic,* May/June 1992.

William E. Phipps, "Cultural Commitments and World Maps," *Focus,* Summer 1991.

Juergen Schulz, "Maps As Metaphors: Mural Map Cycles of the Italian Renaissance," in

David Woodward, ed., *Art and Cartography: Six Historical Essays.* Chicago: University of Chicago Press, 1987.

Norman J. W. Thrower, *Maps and Man: An Examination of Cartography in Relation to Culture and Civilization.* Englewood Cliffs, NJ: Prentice-Hall, 1972.

Wilcomb Washburn, "A New Image of the World," *Unesco Courier,* May 1992.

Denis Wood, "The Power of Maps," *Scientific American,* May 1993.

Index

███

About the Author

■■

Paula Bryant Pratt graduated from Reed College and completed her graduate study at San Diego State University. She has worked in the field of book publishing for more than ten years, as an editorial assistant, a production editor, and as a freelance author and editor. She has also taught community college English composition and creative writing. She is the author of *The Importance of Martha Graham* published by Lucent Books.

Picture Credits

■■

Cover photo by Comstock

Ancient Art and Architecture Collection, 18, 28, 29, 33, 43 (top)

AP/Wide World Photos, 82

Julian Baum/Science Photo Library/Photo Researchers, Inc., 71 (bottom)

The Bettmann Archive, 14

British Museum, 16

© CNES/SPOT Image/Explorer/Photo Researchers, Inc., 70 (bottom)

Culver Pictures, Inc., 15, 17, 23, 51 (bottom), 58, 59 (top)

© Gregory G. Dimijian 1986/Photo Researchers, Inc., 61 (bottom)

Earth Satellite Corporation/Science Photo Library/Photo Researchers, Inc., 70 (top), 77

Barth Falkenberg/Stock Boston, 85

In the Collection of the George Peabody Library, 31 (right), 48, 50, 51 (top), 53, 54 (bottom), 55

Giraudon/Art Resource, NY, 34 (both), 37, 39 (top), 43 (bottom)

Library of Congress, 57, 61 (top)

Gary D. McMichael/Photo Researchers, Inc., 79

NASA/Goddard Institute for Space Studies/Science Photo Library/Photo Researchers, Inc., 80

NASA/Mark Martin/Photo Researchers, Inc., 78

National Maritime Museum, 41

North Wind Picture Archives, 19, 25 (right), 26, 30, 32, 35, 44 (top), 54 (top), 60 (top left and top right), 62

David Parker/Science Photo Library/Photo Researchers, Inc., 72, 73 (left)

Reuters/Bettmann, 73 (right)

Scala, Art Resource, NY, 38, 39 (bottom), 43 (middle)

Stock Montage, Inc., 12, 13, 20 (both), 21, 22, 25 (left), 36, 40 (both), 44 (bottom), 46, 47, 56, 59 (bottom), 60 (bottom)

From Mark Monmonier, *How to Lie with Maps*. Chicago: University of Chicago Press, 1991. Reprinted with permission, 64, 65

Courtesy of the U.S. Geological Survey, 68, 69, 75

© Tom Van Sant/Geosphere Project, Santa Monica/Science Photo Library/Photo Researchers, Inc., 76

Walters Art Gallery, Baltimore, 31 (left)

World Map: Peters Projection. Copyright Akademische Verlagsanstalt. Distributed in North America by Friendship Press. Used by permission, 84

Worldsat International/Science Photo Library/Photo Researchers, Inc., 71 (top)